MICROWAVE
COOKING

MICROWAVE COOKING

JENNY WEBB

CHANCELLOR
PRESS

First published in Great Britain in 1983

This edition published in 1993 by Chancellor Press
an imprint of Reed Consumer Books Limited
Michelin House, 81 Fulham Road, London SW3 6RB
and Auckland, Melbourne, Singapore and Toronto

Copyright © Reed International Books Limited 1983

ISBN 1 85152 451 7

A CIP catalogue record for this book is available from
the British Library

Printed in Hong Kong

CONTENTS

Notes

1. All recipes serve 4 unless otherwise stated.
2. All spoon measurements are level.
3. All eggs are sizes 3 and 4 unless otherwise stated.
4. All sugar is granulated unless otherwise stated.
5. Preparation times given are an average calculated during recipe testing.
6. Metric and imperial measurements have been calculated separately. Use one set of measurements only as they are not exact equivalents.
7. Cooking times may vary slightly depending on the output of the microwave cooker, the type and shape of the container used and the temperature of the food, therefore always observe your manufacturer's instructions.
8. The recipes in this book were tested in a cooker with an output of 700 watts. Food will need to be cooked for a few minutes longer in a cooker with a lower output.

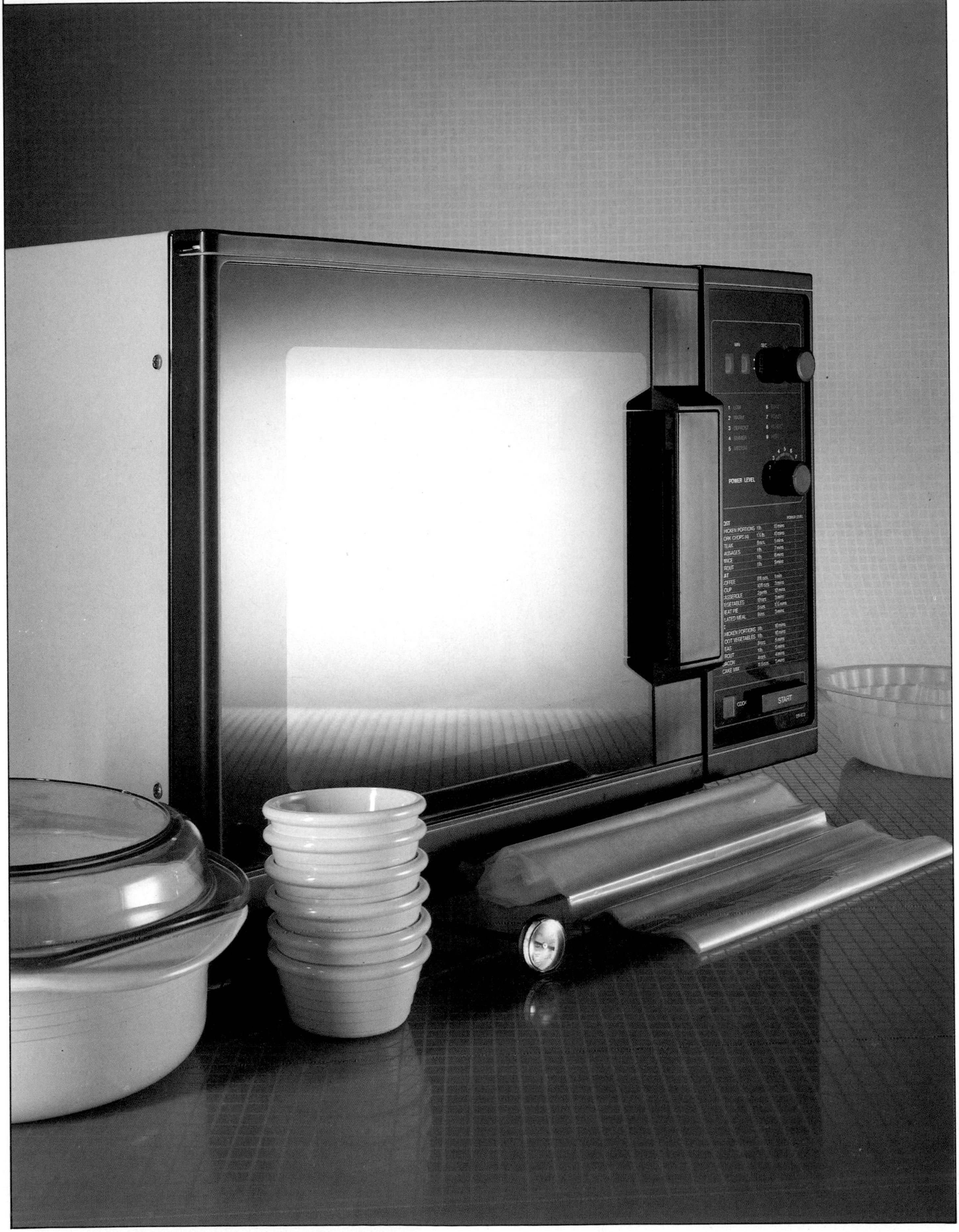
POWER LEVEL
START

INTRODUCTION

The concept of cooking food by microwaves has been experimented with by many scientists throughout the world since before the Second World War. The first microwave cooker was manufactured in the United States in the late 1940s, but it was not until 1955 that a domestic model was produced. In those early days the cookers had small cooking cavities but very large cabinets, were expensive to purchase and limited in what they could do.

The modern domestic microwave cooker is small enough to be positioned on a work surface, yet is so well developed technically that it is able to produce a wide variety of cooked foods to suit individual needs.

The benefits of microwave cooking

The microwave cooker is a small appliance which can be accommodated almost anywhere it is required. No special installation is needed as it can be plugged into a 13 or 15 amp socket. It gives fast results in minutes rather than hours. Running costs are low, because the energy concentrates on the food and not on the surrounding areas. It is a safe appliance to use, as it always remains relatively cool, there are no hot parts on which a user can be burnt, and the kitchen is more comfortable to work in.

Almost any utensil can be used, including paper! Depending upon the size of the cooking cavity, almost any quantity of food from a hamburger to a turkey can be cooked. Since the cooking method retains more nutrients, especially in vegetables, the use of a microwave oven contributes to healthier eating. Foods can also be cooked without fat, so those on a diet can enjoy food without the addition of unwanted calories.

WHAT ARE MICROWAVES?

Microwaves are a form of the electromagnetic energy which is used every day by all of us in one way or another, for example, when we watch television, listen to the radio, have an X-ray or cook food. It is the frequency at which the energy is used which determines the benefits. The microwave cooker is designed to generate electromagnetic waves and these are contained in the cooking cavity.

How microwaves can cook food

To cook raw food conventionally, heat is applied to the outer layer of the food and this gradually penetrates to the centre of the food. Various methods are used to achieve different results. These are known as conduction, convection and radiation. By using one or more of these methods, it is possible to carry out cooking operations, such as boiling, grilling, stewing, frying, baking and roasting. Usually, the heat which cooks the food cannot be seen although the heat source itself can be observed in the form of electricity, gas or coal.

Microwave cooking is an extension of the three basic principles. The microwaves (short waves) are contained in a cooking cavity and cannot be seen. However, they will act in three different ways:

Absorption

Microwaves are attracted to moisture, which is present in all food. Although food looks solid, it is made up of moisture molecules. Once food is placed in the cooking cavity and the microwave energy is switched on, each of the molecules is stimulated and twists back and forth over 2 thousand million times each second. Vibration at such high speed causes the food to heat itself. Unlike conventional cooking, which starts the cooking process on the outer layer of the food, microwaves can penetrate immediately some 4–5 cm/$1\frac{1}{2}$–2 inches all round. Since all the energy is concentrated on cooking the food, the food cooks more quickly than with conventional methods. As a result there is invariably a reduction in energy costs.

Transmission

As microwaves are only attracted to moisture molecules and are absorbed by them, they ignore anything else in the cooking cavity and pass through many other materials as if they were invisible. It is rather like sitting in a car on a warm day, with the sun streaming through the window. The warmth of the sun can be felt but the car windows remain cool. Microwaves act in the same manner and are not attracted by internal cooker material, only food.

Reflection

Although microwaves are absorbed by food and pass through such materials as glass, china, wood, paper and plastic, they are reflected by metal. Since the walls of the cooking cavity are of metal, the microwaves reflect off the walls, creating an invisible energy pattern which contributes to a good energy distribution in the cavity. This also means that if food were to be placed in a metal container it would be screened from the microwaves and would not cook.

It is rather like bouncing a ball against a solid wall – it will always bounce back. If a hole was made in the wall, the ball would continue to travel through it.

THE BASIC CONTROLS

Microwave cookers have a variety of controls, in the form of buttons, dials or touch-sensitive pads. However, all models will have a timer and cook control. In addition, many include a defrost control and possibly a variable power control to allow slower cooking.

The timer

Timing is an essential part of cooking by microwaves. Once the timer has been set, and the cooking control switched on, cooking will continue until the timer automatically switches off the microwave energy. When it stops, it will indicate completion by a ping, buzz or light. Should you need to get to the food during the cooking, open the door and the timed sequence will halt. Shut the door again and the cooker will continue without needing to be reset.

The cook control

This is also sometimes known as the on/off control. It generally works in conjunction with the timer. The majority of cookers have this control but in one or two makes the microwave energy is simply generated by the closing of the cooker door and similarly switches off once the door is opened.

The defrost control

This control is for thawing frozen food fast and, once set, will automatically reduce the microwave energy being applied to the food. Depending upon the model selected, it may either reduce the wattage or pulse the energy on and off. It is a particularly useful feature for thawing large items of food as it ensures an even thaw but prevents food from cooking. A further benefit is to use the control for cooking foods slowly; the energy will cycle on and off alternately in accordance with the selected setting, thus slowing the cooking process down. When using this control the timer is set for longer, as directed in specific recipes. For other foods, unless instructions are given in the manufacturer's handbook, the exact timing will have to be judged by experience.

Variable power control

This control is simply a method of enabling the user to select more or less microwave energy to suit his or her particular cooking needs. As a dimmer switch for light gives a choice of lighting levels, so the microwave energy can be adjusted. There is no standardization of settings between models, but the instruction book supplied with individual cookers gives both recipes and guidance as to which setting is best suited for a specific cooking operation. Like the defrost control, the timer is set and the cooker will automatically adjust to the selected cooking level.

SITING THE MICROWAVE COOKER

The average microwave cooker is about the size of a television and only requires a 13 or 15 amp socket. It can be placed in almost any position and in any room (excluding the bathroom). It may be accommodated on a table top, built in or even placed on a trolley, so that it can be moved at any time to the most convenient working position. Because it is a 'cool' appliance, it is particularly beneficial to the disabled or elderly.

Since air is drawn in by a fan to cool the magnetron, the air inlet grills must not be blocked and the cooker should not be placed near an appliance where this air is likely to be hot, e.g. near a hob. The magnetron is often referred to as the 'heart' of the cooker, as this component generates the microwave energy.

SAFETY

Microwave cookers are as safe as any other electrical appliance in the home and must comply with the appropriate government legislation. However, for reassurance, it is worth buying a model which carries the BEAB (British Electrotechnical Approvals Board) label. This confirms that the model meets the requirements of the appropriate British Standard for electrical safety and microwave leakage levels.

COOKING CONTAINERS AND UTENSILS

Cooking utensils for the microwave cooker include not only solid shapes like bowls, jugs and casseroles, but also bags, cling film and paper. Practically any material can be used. There are a few exceptions related to metal, and a few plastic materials.

Although microwaves will generally not damage cooking utensils, it is important to remember that the heat of the food may sometimes do so. For example, syrup heated in a glass utensil would reach such a high temperature that the glass could not withstand it.

Metal utensils

Unless the cooker manufacturer confirms its use, metal in any form should not be used. China decorated with metal, lead crystal, or any material which contains metal, such as metal ties used for securing roasting bags, are not suitable. Nor are small pieces of foil or shallow foil containers, unless recommended. Metal can cause 'arcing' (i.e. sparking) and may result in the walls inside the cooker becoming pitted.

China, ceramic and oven-to-tableware utensils

Make sure that containers do not have metal trim or pattern as this will cause arcing (check for gold or silver printing on the underside) and that any handles have not been glued on. The use of antique china should be avoided. Porous pottery is not really suitable for microwave cooking. Moisture absorbed in the pottery itself will heat up, making the container hot – unlike most microwave containers which remain cool – and this absorption will slow down the cooking of the foods by an unknown and variable amount.

Glass utensils

Glass such as tumblers, coupe dishes and small dishes are suitable, but should not be used in recipes where the food is likely to reach such a high temperature that they may crack. Food containing a high proportion of sugar or fat should not be cooked in glass for this reason. Do not use glass with metal decoration or made of lead crystal. Never leave a thermometer in the bowl while cooking preserves.

Plastic and paper utensils

There are several proprietary paper or plastic containers designed for microwave cooking. Providing the plastic can withstand the food temperature it will be satisfactory. This includes boil-in-the-bags, polythene cling film and roasting bags. Thick polythene bags could be used for short-term heating, but preferably not for foods with high fat or sugar content. Avoid melaware (melamine cups, plates, kitchen tools) as these can taint food.

Kitchen paper, greaseproof and cardboard can be used but those which appear to have a wax finish, which could melt from the heat of the food, should not.

Never line a browning dish or skillet with cling film or kitchen paper as they could scorch or burn due to the high temperatures reached by the container.

Wood and basketry utensils

Wooden utensils or baskets may be placed in the microwave cooker but only for a short time. Do not use baskets which have been bonded with glue or have wire or staples used in their construction.

Utensil and cooking advice

Unlike conventional cooking, many utensils can be used, including cups, mugs, tumblers, cardboard boxes lined with polythene cling film or greaseproof paper, bowls, basins and casseroles. Choose the right shape for the cooking operation, remembering that round dishes give better results than square ones. Shallow dishes are better than deep ones.

Avoid cooking cakes in a square or oblong container as the food in the corners may overcook and become dry. Ring-shaped utensils will frequently give a better cooked result with many cake mixtures.

Although not essential, choose a container in which the food may be spread evenly, and be evenly exposed to the action of the microwaves. A utensil which is narrower at one end will cook the food more quickly in the narrow area.

When heating liquids, choose a container large enough to avoid boiling over: glasses should be strong enough to withstand the temperature of the heated liquid. When thawing liquid-based foods, such as soups, place the frozen block in a tight-fitting utensil, so that the thawed liquid is retained close to the frozen block.

Cover foods which need to have the moisture within them to cook the food, for example, stews, soups, fish, peeled fruit, vegetables, steamed puddings, frozen foods. Polythene cling film can be used as a cover, as can plates or casserole lids.

Do not cover foods which are intended to be 'dry', for example, cakes, pastry, fruit and vegetables in skins and bread products.

COOKING INSTRUCTIONS

Sometimes instructions are given which may seen unnecessary. As with any cooking operation, the cook is in control, but there are reasons behind instructions. *Stir liquids*, such as soups and stews. The other areas of the liquid are getting more exposure to microwave energy. Therefore by stirring, the liquid will heat more evenly. In the case of sauces, stirring will help to avoid lumps.

Rearrange food. Unevenly shaped foods, such as chops or fish, may cook more quickly in some parts. By rearranging, for example, turning over the food or changing its position, this can be checked.

Turn over large foods like joints and poultry. As these foods tend to be irregular in shape, the exposure will vary across the food; by turning over, a more even cooking result can be achieved.

Turn around containers. This instruction can be particularly beneficial when cooking cakes, as it will contribute to an even rise.

Set aside, covered or *leave to stand, covered*. After cooking, the food is left to stand for a specific number of minutes. This is not done in order to keep food warm but because foods continue to cook by conduction once the microwave energy has been switched off. Therefore, to avoid dehydration, some foods benefit from being left to stand before serving. This is particularly important with large joints of meat, some cakes and puddings.

Prick or score any food with a skin or membrane, e.g. unpeeled apples, jacket potatoes, whole tomatoes, sausages or egg yolks. This simple precaution prevents the food from bursting.

Stand or an upturned plate. This instruction usually relates to cooking cakes or large joints of meat and helps to cook the centre of the food.

PRINCIPLES OF MICROWAVE COOKING

By following certain principles when cooking conventionally, a better result will be achieved. The same applies to microwave cooking.

Timing

Timing plays a much more important part in the cooked results obtained from a microwave cooker than in conventional cooking. It is wise to undercook, check, and return the food to continue cooking. Overcooking or heating will dehydrate the food and render it unpalatably tough or hard.

The quantity of food that can be cooked in one operation relates to the cooking time. For example, one jacket potato may take 5 minutes to cook but two take 8 minutes. This is simply because the level of microwave energy remains the same and has to be distributed amongst an increased quantity of food.

The positioning of food

Since the lowest activity of microwave energy is next to the walls, in the corners and absolute centre of the cooking cavity, it is better to place the food off-centre on the floor, unless otherwise directed by the cooker manufacturer.

The more microwave energy exposure the food can get, the more evenly and quickly it is cooked. This is particularly beneficial for small individual items of foods. For example, items such as small cakes or potatoes should be arranged in a circle with a space between each. For food such as chops, they are best arranged with the thinner areas pointing to the middle of the utensil.

Browning food

When cooking conventionally with a heat source, the outer layer of food which is exposed to heat changes colour as it 'burns'. In cooking processes where no heat is directly applied, such as steaming or microwave cooking, the food does not brown. Microwave energy heats and cooks food but as there is no external application of heat and because it cooks so quickly, browning in the accepted manner does not occur.

Browning is not required for all foods, for example, fruit and vegetables. Nevertheless, meat and poultry do usually require some degree of browning to make them acceptable to the eye.

Because large joints of meat and poultry need a longer cooking time, the surface area of fat starts to change colour: it may result in an acceptable colour but it will not be as crisp or as brown as meat cooked conventionally.

There are several methods available which enable the food to benefit from speedy and economical cooking yet retain visual appeal.

- After microwave cooking, brown the food under a pre-heated conventional grill or in a frying pan.
- Use a microwave browning dish. This is specially designed to absorb microwave energy over the base. Once preheated, the base is hot enough to sear food before cooking.
- Should colour be the requirement rather than a crisp skin, the meat can be brushed with a colourful sauce, such as tomato sauce, to liven up its appearance.

MAINTENANCE

Like all appliances, if the manufacturer's instructions are followed, little or no maintenance is required. However, the majority of manufacturers offer a maintenance service, the cost of which can be discussed at the time of purchase. It is important that at no time should anyone but a fully trained microwave service engineer dismantle the cooker or endeavour to carry out a repair.

The manufacturer's instruction book should always be referred to but in general:

- Any soil or spillage should be wiped clean with a damp cloth after use.
- An abrasive cleaning agent must not be used on any part of the cooker.
- A sharp implement, such as a knife, must never be used to remove hardened food, especially in the area of the door seal.
- A cup of water placed in the cavity will absorb any microwaves if the cooker is turned on accidentally.

USING THE RECIPES

The recipes in this book have been tested in a cooker with a maximum output of 700 watts. Those who have a microwave cooker of a lower output may find it necessary in some instances to increase the cooking time slightly. Before doing so, check the food at the time given in the recipe. Only then should any additional cooking time be considered.

All the food used in the recipes was at room temperature. Should food be used from the refrigerator or quantities increased, then a slightly longer cooking time may be required.

Any suitable container may be used for the recipes but to aid in the cooking of a recipe, a container size has been specified. In some instances, a general description has been given. For guidance:

Large bowl – 2.75 litre ($4\frac{1}{2}$–5 pint)
Medium bowl – 2 litre ($3\frac{1}{2}$ pint)
Small bowl – 1.2 litre (2 pint)
Small jug – 600 ml (1 pint)
Large jug – 1 litre ($1\frac{3}{4}$ pint)

When covering food, cling film has been used, but a plate or casserole lid may be substituted.

Generally, it does not matter what type of utensil is used for stirring, etc., provided that, if it is metal, it is not left in the cooker cavity during the actual cooking.

All food is cooked uncovered unless otherwise stated in the recipes.

SOUPS

Making soup in the microwave is so simple, and needs very few utensils. A large bowl is usually all that is required to produce enough soup for four. Unlike conventional methods, the vegetables, meat or fish for microwave soup are cooked in little or no water before any large quantity of stock is added. Also, as the soup cooks so quickly, very little evaporation occurs; so if a conventional recipe is used, the liquid can frequently be reduced.

Although the microwave cooks extremely quickly, an electric kettle uses less energy and is quicker to use if heating more than 600 ml (1 pint) water; therefore, hot stock rather than cold is used for soups.

EGGS AND CHEESE

Eggs are always sensitive to heat and cooking with microwave energy is no different. However, a successful cooked product can be achieved if several points are considered before-hand. The egg size will make the difference to the cooking time, so if different sized eggs are used, the timing will vary. An egg, at room temperature, will cook more quickly than one straight from the refrigerator. Always remove eggs from the microwave before they look completely cooked, then stand for a minute or two before serving. To avoid the yolk bursting, it should be pricked before cooking. Most forms of eggs can be cooked, but eggs in shells must never be attempted as the shells may burst and cause damage to the cooker interior.

When adding eggs to sauces, it is well worth cooking for seconds rather than minutes and to check the food frequently to avoid overcooking. Delicate egg dishes, such as egg custards, are likely to be better if cooked on a lower setting or with the dish standing in another dish of water, as this slows the cooking time down. Conventionally hard-boiled eggs go tough and rubbery, but they can be used in a recipe providing care is taken that they are not overheated. Finally, always refer to the microwave manufacturer's book for any further guidance.

Like eggs, cheese is sensitive to heat and requires careful attention. Grated or sliced cheese melts very quickly and if overcooked will become stringy, so it is better to time in seconds rather than minutes. As there is no heat source, the cheese will not brown; should this not be acceptable brown the cooked dish under a conventional grill or sprinkled with a ground spice.

When adding cheese to cooked sauces, it is not usually necessary to cook the sauce further. Simply stir the cheese into the hot sauce until it melts.

MEAT AND FISH

The microwave cooker will be of tremendous value in preparing main dishes of meat and fish. It can thaw and/or reheat food very quickly, so a meal can easily be made almost straight from the freezer.

It is accepted that certain meats will not brown, but as explained on page 10 this can be easily remedied by utilising the microwave cooker for high speed cooking and a conventional grill for finishing.

Most meat, poultry, offal and fish cook very well in the microwave and frequently, due to the speed of cooking, less shrinkage occurs. Some cookers have the facility of slowing down the cooking time, and in these it is possible to obtain good results with the cheaper cuts of meat.

The following charts give a guide to meat and fish cooking times. Remember that it is better to cook for the shorter time first, check the meat for readiness, and return it to the oven if necessary.

FISH

Fish and Weight	Approx Cooking time Full/Maximum (cook, covered)	Standing Time (covered)
Cod Fillets 450g/1lb	4 mins.	5–10 mins.
Cod Steaks 450g/1lb	4 mins.	5–10 mins.
Cod Fillets, smoked 450g/1lb	4–5 mins.	5–10 mins.
Plaice, gutted and filleted 450g/1lb	3 mins.	5–10 mins.
Sole, filleted 450g/1lb	3–4 mins.	5–10 mins.
Haddock gutted and filleted 450g/1lb	3 mins.	5–10 mins.
Mackerel (?), gutted but whole 225g/8oz	2 mins. each side	5–10 mins.
Trout (?), gutted but whole 225g/8oz	2 mins. each side	5 mins.
Kipper Fillets 225g/8oz	3 mins.	5 mins.

SMALL CUTS OF MEAT

Cut or Type of Meat and Weight	Special Points	Approx Cooking Time Full/Maximum	Standing Time (covered)
Mince: 450g/1lb	Cook covered	5 mins.	2 mins.
Steak: Rump or Fillet 225g/8oz		3–4 mins.	2 mins.
Chops, loin: Lamb or Pork 2 portions 150g/5oz each		6 mins.	2 mins.
Chops, chump: Lamb or Pork 300g/11oz	Sprinkle with microwave seasoning before cooking	7 mins.	2 mins.
Fillet: Lamb or Pork 350g/12oz	Cook covered	6 mins.	5 mins.
Breast of Lamb: 560g/1lb 4oz	Cook on roasting rack, sprinkle with browning agent	6 mins.	3 mins.
Bacon: 225g/8oz	Cook on rack	4 mins.	2 mins.
Chicken: 2 portions 400g/14oz each	Cook on a rack to allow fat to drain. Sprinkle with browning agent	10 mins.	10–15 mins.
Gammon steaks: 2 portions 200g/7oz each	Cook covered	2½–3 mins.	5 mins.
Gammon joints: 450g/1lb	Cook covered	7 mins.	10 mins.
Liver: 450g/1lb		4 mins.	5 mins.
Kidneys: 2 or 3	Slice before cooking	3–5 mins.	5 mins.

SPECIAL POINT FOR ALL MEAT: Meat cooking temperatures are calculated per pound weight.

NOTE: The charts are for guidance only – always refer to the actual recipe instruction in preference to the charts where available.

JOINTS

Joint and Weight	Approx Cooking time per 450g/1lb Full/Maximum	Standing Time (wrapped tightly in foil)
Beef: 450g/1lb	Rare: 4–5 mins. Medium: 7 mins. Well done: 9 mins.	20–30 mins.
Lamb: 450g/1lb	7–9 mins.	25–30 mins.
Pork: 450g/1lb	7–9 mins.	20–25 mins.
Gammon joints: 450g/1lb	7 mins.	15–20 mins.
Chicken: 450g/1lb	6–7 mins.	15–20 mins.
Turkey: up to 3.6kg/8lb	6–7 mins.	25–30 mins.

VEGETABLES

Virtually any fresh vegetables can be cooked in a microwave, and the results are first class in colour, taste and crisp texture. In general, the container is covered and very little water is used, as the moisture within the vegetable is sufficient. Salt should not be sprinkled directly on to the vegetables before cooking as this can result in dehydration and toughness, so add salt to the cooking water or use to season the vegetable after cooking. Old root vegetables, such as carrots, will not improve with microwave cooking – the lack of moisture simply contributes to greater dehydration and the vegetable becomes tough and hard. The chart gives a guide to preparation and cooking times of fresh vegetables.

Frozen vegetables cook quickly, too, and the result is excellent, but it is wise to refer to the manufacturer's cooking times to ensure the best results.

FRESH VEGETABLES

Fresh Vegetable and Weight	Preparation	Water to be added	Approx Cooking Time Full/Maximum
Artichokes, 4 medium	Wash and trim	150ml/¼ pint	10–20 mins.
Aubergines 450g/1lb	Peel and dice	2 tablespoons	5–6 mins.
Beetroot 450g/1lb	Wash, skin and cut in half	None	7–8 mins.
Broad beans 450g/1lb	Remove from pods and wash	2 tablespoons	7–10 mins.
Broccoli 225g/8oz	Prepare, slice into spears	3 tablespoons	4–5 mins.
Brussels Sprouts 225g/8oz	Trim	3–4 tablespoons	7–8 mins.
Cabbage 450g/1lb	Trim and shred	3 tablespoons	7–8 mins.
Carrots 225g/8oz	Scrape and slice	2 tablespoons	6–7 mins.
Cauliflower 450g/1lb	Trim and cut in florets	4 tablespoons	9–10 mins.
Celery, 1 head	Trim and dice	150ml/¼ pint	10–13 mins.
Corn on the Cob (2)	Trim and wash	4 tablespoons	7–8 mins.
Courgettes 450g/1lb	Trim, slice, sprinkle lightly with salt	None	7–9 mins.
Leeks 450g/1lb	Trim and slice	3 tablespoons	7–9 mins.
Mushrooms, button 110g/4oz	Peel or wash, leave whole	2 tablespoons	2½–3 mins.
Parsnips 450g/1lb	Peel and slice	3 tablespoons	6–8 mins.
Peas 225g/8oz	Remove from pods and wash	3 tablespoons	6–8 mins.
Potatoes, boiled 450g/1lb	Peel and cut into evenly sized pieces	3 tablespoons	6–7 mins.
Potatoes, jacket (2) 225–275g/8oz–10oz	Scrub and prick well	None	9 mins.
Runner beans 225g/8oz	String and slice	4 tablespoons	6–7 mins.
Spinach 225g/8oz	Wash and shred	None	6–8 mins.
Swede 225g/8oz	Peel and dice	None	6–8 mins.
Tomatoes 225g/8oz	Slice	None	2–3 mins.
Turnips 225g/8oz	Peel and dice	2 tablespoons	6–7 mins.

SPECIAL POINTS FOR ALL VEGETABLES. Place vegetables in a bowl. Add required amount of water. Cook covered. Leave to stand, covered, for 2 mins., after cooking or for the time stated in the actual recipe, strain and season to taste.

RICE, PULSES AND PASTA

The microwave can be used most successfully for cooking rice and pasta. However, the method requires a large quantity of water, and it is more economical and quicker to boil this in a kettle rather than to use the microwave cooker. The rice or pasta must be left to stand, covered, for some minutes after the cooking time and this can be useful if a sauce is to be prepared. To achieve the best results, a very large, covered container should be used. The addition of a little oil will prevent the water boiling over.

If making a rice milk pudding, it is better to use a lower setting and an extra large container. It must also be remembered that as there is no external heat, the top of the pudding will not change colour to the same degree as that produced by conventional cooking. If a fairly thick rice pudding is desired, remove the cover three-quarters of the way through cooking.

The advice given on cooking pulses in the microwave is varied, and it is advisable to check the manufacturer's instruction book for guidance as to the method, time and setting required. The result of the cooked product does tend to vary (it sometimes can still have a 'bite' to it) depending on the pulse, quantity and method used. If cooking red kidney beans, use the full setting and ensure that the beans are rigorously boiled for at least 10 minutes.

PUDDINGS AND CAKES

British puddings are superb but most take rather a long time to cook and as a consequence tend to be left out of many daily menus. However, the speed of the microwave enables perfect puddings to be produced in minutes rather than hours. When reheating a pudding with a high sugar/fat/alcohol content, it is advisable to check frequently as very high temperatures can be reached very quickly. Be careful not to overcook the mixture and be in attendance throughout the operation.

Steamed puddings cook in their own moisture, and this does away with the inconvenience of steaming pans on a hob and the ever constant need to replenish water. Fruit is cooked to perfection in little or no water and retains both shape and vivid colours.

Pastry is less successful, and only a shortcrust pastry flan case or suet pudding are likely to be acceptable. Nevertheless, a great deal of time and money can be saved by cooking at high speed.

Cooking cakes in the microwave is an area where much will depend upon the recipe and the expectations of the cook. Often a better result can be obtained if self-raising flour is used and an extra tablespoon or two of liquid is added to the mixture. Containers can be greased or lined, but greasing and flouring results in a rather unpleasant film of flour on the outside of the cooked product. Cakes will not brown, so unless the cake mixture is a coloured one, such as chocolate, some form of decoration will be required to give the cake eye appeal.

DRINKS AND PRESERVES

The microwave cooker is ideal for heating up cold coffee or chocolate and even for tea, providing, of course, the cups have no metal decoration. It can even be used to make tea in the teapot! Just place the water in the teapot, bring to the boil and add the tea. The microwave is also useful for making warming drinks, such as mulled wine and cider, or even a hot liqueur coffee to follow a special meal. It is worth remembering, if heating milk, to choose a cup or mug large enough to avoid boiling over and glasses that are able to withstand the temperature of the heated liquid.

Jams and chutneys cooked in the microwave take on a special flavour and, compared to those cooked conventionally, are even more colourful. For small quantities of preserves, the microwave cooker is ideal because there is no risk of scorching or burning. However, if very large quantities are to be made, it may be more convenient and cheaper to use the conventional methods.

Making jam and chutney in the microwave follows the usual principles of preserving, but it is important to use a very large utensil to avoid any boiling over, to use a cloth when handling the utensil and never to leave a thermometer in the utensil whilst cooking.

SAUCES

Once sauces have been made in a microwave cooker it is unlikely that any other method will ever be used again. There are so many advantages with the microwave: the sauce can be made in the serving jug (provided it isn't metal or metal-rimmed), often all the ingredients can be blended together before cooking, lumpy sauces are less likely, and there is no opportunity to scorch or burn the sauce. A further advantage is the speed and convenience of reheating sauces, so many can be made in advance, thus giving more time to preparing the rest of the meal.

USING THE MICROWAVE

In thinking about your new microwave cooker, the main thing to remember is that it is simply another appliance in the kitchen which does not *have* to be used for every cooking operation. It can be used instead of, or in conjunction with, conventional cookers – to suit your needs and preferences. It is a very fast cooking appliance, but even with such speed it still takes some time, and this must be taken into consideration in planning a menu.

Many foods such as sauces, gravies and casseroles, can be cooked in advance and then reheated when required. A hot snack can be cooked in minutes, by even a junior member of a family, and supper dish prepared without the expense of heating a large oven for a comparatively small quantity of food. A further bonus is that the food can be cooked and/or reheated in the serving dish, or even as individual portions. This is particularly handy if someone is expected late for dinner.

Throughout the chapters in this book you will find various planned menus, together with an 'order of cooking'. These will give you guidance in using the microwave cooker for complete menu planning and take you through all the stages of providing a delicious meal for family and friends.

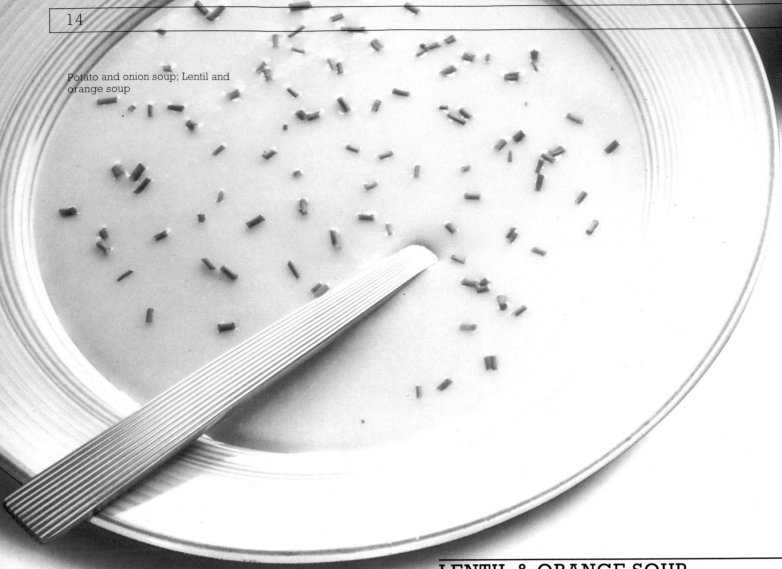

Potato and onion soup; Lentil and orange soup

LENTIL & ORANGE SOUP

Preparation time: about 10 minutes Cooking time: about 27 minutes
Microwave setting: Maximum (Full)

25 g (1 oz) butter
100 g (4 oz) split red lentils
1 onion, peeled and finely
   chopped
1 celery stick, finely sliced
½ medium carrot, peeled
   and grated
¼ teaspoon dried thyme
900 ml (1½ pints) hot
   chicken stock

150 ml (¼ pint) orange juice
grated rind of ½ orange
bay leaf
salt
freshly ground black
   pepper
orange rind, to garnish

1. Place the butter and lentils in a large bowl. Cover and cook for 2 minutes, stirring halfway through.
2. Stir in the onion, celery, carrot and thyme. Cover and cook for 7 minutes, stirring halfway through.
3. Stir in 600 ml (1 pint) of the hot stock with the orange juice, rind, bay leaf, salt and pepper. Cover. Cook for 10 minutes, stirring halfway through cooking.
4. Remove the bay leaf and stir in the remaining hot stock. Cool slightly.
5. Pour the soup into a liquidizer and blend.
6. Return to the bowl and reheat for 8 minutes. Adjust the seasoning and garnish with orange.

POTATO & ONION SOUP

Preparation time: about 10 minutes Cooking time: about 17½ minutes
Microwave setting: Maximum (Full)

275 g (10 oz) onions,
   peeled and finely
   chopped
750 g (1½ lb) potatoes,
   peeled and thinly sliced
1 teaspoon dried mixed
   herbs
600 ml (1 pint) milk

salt
300 ml (½ pint) hot beef
   stock
freshly ground black
   pepper
2 teaspoons chopped
   chives, to garnish

1. Place the onions and potatoes in a large bowl, cover and cook for 13 minutes, stirring halfway through cooking.
2. Stir in the herbs, milk and salt. Cover and cook for 4½ minutes, stirring halfway through cooking.
3. Stir in the hot beef stock, pepper and more salt, if necessary, to taste. Purée in a blender or food processor.
4. Pour into 4 soup bowls and garnish.

SOUPS

COUNTRY VEGETABLE SOUP

Preparation time: about 15 minutes Cooking time: about 20 minutes
Microwave setting: Maximum (Full)

25 g (1 oz) butter
100 g (4 oz) cabbage, finely
   shredded
100 g (4 oz) potatoes,
   peeled and diced
100 g (4 oz) onions, peeled
   and chopped
100 g (4 oz) carrots, peeled
   and thinly sliced
50 g (2 oz) red pepper,
   cored, seeded and diced

50 g (2 oz) turnip, peeled
   and diced
1 / 400 g (14 oz) can
   tomatoes with juice
salt
freshly ground black
   pepper
900 ml (1½ pints) hot beef
   stock

1. Place the butter, cabbage, potatoes, onions, carrots, red pepper, turnip, tomatoes, salt and pepper in a large bowl. Cover and cook for 10 minutes, stirring halfway through cooking.
2. Stir in the stock. Cover and cook for 10 minutes or until the vegetables are tender, stirring halfway through cooking.
3. Taste and adjust the seasoning before serving.

TOMATO SOUP WITH RICE & BASIL

Preparation time: about 5 minutes Cooking time: about 14 minutes
Microwave setting: Maximum (Full)

25 g (1 oz) butter
1 large onion, peeled and
   chopped
40 g (1½ oz) plain flour
2 tablespoons tomato
   purée
750 g (1½ lb) ripe tomatoes,
   cut into quarters
¼ teaspoon celery salt
1 teaspoon caster sugar
1 teaspoon dried basil

salt
freshly ground black
   pepper
300 ml (½ pint) milk
450 ml (¾ pint) hot chicken
   stock
4 tablespoons cooked rice
2 tablespoons single
   cream, to serve
   (optional)

1. Place the butter and onion in a large bowl. Cover and cook for 4 minutes.
2. Stir in the flour, tomato purée, tomatoes, celery salt, sugar, basil, salt and pepper. Add the milk. Cover and cook for 10 minutes, stirring halfway through cooking.
3. Add the hot stock and allow to cool slightly.
4. Pour the soup into a liquidizer and blend until smooth.
5. Sieve the liquidized soup to remove the tomato skins and pips. Stir in the cooked rice.
6. Return the soup to the bowl and reheat uncovered for 3–4 minutes. Adjust the seasoning.
7. Serve the soup with a swirl of cream floating on the top, if liked.

Country vegetable soup; Tomato
soup with rice and basil

FISH SOUP

Preparation time: about 20 minutes Cooking time: about 17½ minutes
Microwave setting: Maximum (Full)

1 onion, peeled and finely
  chopped
1 small green pepper,
  cored, seeded and finely
  diced
225 g (8 oz) potatoes,
  peeled and finely diced
1 tablespoon oil
1 garlic clove, peeled and
  crushed
½ teaspoon dried rosemary

1 teaspoon chopped fresh
  parsley
salt
2 bay leaves
600 ml (1 pint) cold water
750 g (1½ lb) filleted white
  fish, cut into small pieces
450 ml (¾ pint) hot water
freshly ground black
  pepper

1. Place the onion, green pepper, potatoes, oil,
garlic, rosemary, parsley and salt in a large bowl.
Cover and cook for 7½ minutes or until the
vegetables are tender.
2. Stir in the bay leaves, cold water and fish. Cover
and cook for 10 minutes, stirring halfway through.
3. Stir the hot water gently into the fish mixture.
4. Remove the bay leaves. Taste and adjust the
seasoning, then serve in individual soup bowls.

PEA & MINT SOUP

Preparation time: about 5 minutes Cooking time: about 19 minutes
Microwave setting: Maximum (Full)

Serves 4–5

25 g (1 oz) butter
1 medium onion, peeled
  and finely chopped
450 g (1 lb) frozen peas
1 tablespoon chopped
  fresh mint
600 ml (1 pint) hot chicken
  stock

salt
freshly ground black
  pepper
25 g (1 oz) plain flour
450 ml (¾ pint) milk
4 mint sprigs, to garnish

1. Place the butter, onion, peas and mint in a large
bowl. Cover and cook for 8 minutes, stirring halfway
through cooking.
2. Add the hot chicken stock, salt and pepper. Cover
and cook for 5 minutes.
3. Place the flour in a small bowl and gradually
blend in the milk. Stir the milk into the soup.
4. Pour the soup into a liquidizer and blend until
smooth.
5. Return the soup to the bowl, cover and cook for 6
minutes, stirring halfway through cooking.
6. Taste and adjust the seasoning, then serve
garnished with sprigs of mint.

Fish soup; Pea and mint soup

LETTUCE SOUP WITH CROÛTONS

Preparation time: about 5 minutes Cooking time: about 19 minutes
Microwave setting: Maximum (Full)

1 medium onion, peeled
  and finely chopped
50 g (2 oz) butter
25 g (1 oz) plain flour
450 ml ($\frac{3}{4}$ pint) hot chicken
  stock
300 ml ($\frac{1}{2}$ pint) milk
225 g (8 oz) lettuce leaves,
  washed and chopped
$\frac{1}{4}$ teaspoon grated nutmeg

$\frac{1}{4}$ teaspoon caster sugar
salt
freshly ground black
  pepper
1 egg yolk

Croûtons:
2 slices fresh white bread,
  cut into cubes
4 tablespoons oil

1. Place the onion and butter in a large bowl. Cover
and cook for 4 minutes.
2. Stir in the flour, hot stock, milk, lettuce, nutmeg,
sugar, salt and pepper. Cover and cook for 9
minutes. Cool slightly.
3. Pour the soup and the egg yolk into a liquidizer
and blend until smooth.
4. Return soup to the bowl. Reheat for 2 minutes.
5. Taste and adjust the seasoning, then serve
garnished with croûtons.
6. To make the croûtons, toss the cubes of bread in
the oil. Spread the cubes over a plate. Cook for 2
minutes. Stir and cook for a further 2 minutes,
checking and stirring the croûtons frequently until
browned. Drain on paper towels.

CHICKEN & VEGETABLE SOUP

Preparation time: about 15 minutes Cooking time: about 26 minutes
Microwave setting: Maximum (Full)

1 carrot, peeled and finely
  sliced
1 medium potato, peeled
  and diced
2 button mushrooms, sliced
1 small red pepper, cored,
  seeded and diced
1 small turnip, peeled and
  diced
$\frac{1}{2}$ leek, trimmed and finely
  sliced

1 small onion, peeled and
  chopped
600 g (1$\frac{1}{4}$ lb) chicken pieces
1 litre (1$\frac{3}{4}$ pints) hot chicken
  stock
salt
freshly ground black
  pepper
bouquet garni

1. Place the carrot, potato, mushrooms, red pepper,
turnip, leek and onion in a large bowl. Place the
chicken pieces on top of the vegetables. Cover and
cook for 15 minutes, stirring halfway through.
2. Add the hot chicken stock, salt, pepper and
bouquet garni. Cover and cook for 8 minutes.
3. Take out the chicken. Remove and discard the
skin, then cut the flesh from the bones. Chop the
chicken flesh and return it to the soup.
4. Remove the bouquet garni. Reheat for 3 minutes.
Taste and adjust the seasoning, before serving.

Lettuce soup with croûtons;
Chicken and vegetable soup

VICHYSSOISE

Preparation time: about 10 minutes, plus chilling
Cooking time: about 14 minutes Microwave setting: Maximum (Full)

Serves 4–5

350 g (12 oz) potatoes, peeled and thinly sliced
750 g (1½ lb) leeks, trimmed and thinly sliced
1 celery stick, finely chopped
50 g (2 oz) butter
4 tablespoons water
900 ml (1½ pints) hot chicken stock
salt
freshly ground black pepper
150–300 ml (¼–½ pint) double cream
1 tablespoon chopped fresh chives, to garnish

1. Place the potatoes, leeks, celery, butter and water in a large bowl. Cover and cook for 8 minutes, stirring halfway through cooking.
2. Add half the stock, salt and pepper. Cover and cook for 6 minutes. Add the remaining stock.
3. Pour the soup into a liquidizer and blend.
4. Sieve the liquidized soup. Taste and adjust the seasoning.
5. Allow to cool completely, then chill for 2 hours.
6. Before serving, stir in the cream and garnish with chopped chives.

MUSHROOM SOUP

Preparation time: 5–10 minutes Cooking time: about 12½ minutes
Microwave setting: Maximum (Full)

25 g (1 oz) butter
1 medium onion, peeled and finely chopped
225 g (8 oz) flat mushrooms, chopped
25 g (1 oz) plain flour
300 ml (½ pint) milk
salt
freshly ground black pepper
600 ml (1 pint) hot chicken stock
4 tablespoons single cream
2 button mushrooms, thinly sliced, to garnish

1. Place the butter and onion in a large bowl, cover and cook for 5 minutes. Stir in the chopped mushrooms, cover and cook for 3 minutes.
2. Stir in the flour, then gradually blend in the milk. Season to taste with salt and pepper. Cover and cook for 2½ minutes.
3. Stir in the hot stock. Purée in a blender or food processor, then pour back into the bowl.
4. Taste and adjust the seasoning. Stir in the cream. Reheat, uncovered, for 3 minutes if required.
5. Pour into 4 soup bowls and garnish with the sliced mushrooms.

Vichyssoise; Mushroom soup

Globe artichokes with French
dressing; Mushrooms in garlic
butter

STARTERS

GLOBE ARTICHOKES WITH FRENCH DRESSING

Preparation time: about 10 minutes, plus cooling
Cooking time: about 20 minutes Microwave setting: Maximum (Full)

4 globe artichokes
300 ml (½ pint) water
1 tablespoon lemon juice

French dressing:
salt

freshly ground black
  pepper
1 teaspoon dry mustard
6 tablespoons wine vinegar
175 ml (6 fl oz) olive oil

1. Using a pair of scissors, snip off the point from each of the outer leaves of the artichokes. Cut the stalks from the bases. Rinse the artichokes and turn upside down to drain.
2. Pour the water and lemon juice into a large shallow dish. Cook for 4 minutes.
3. Stand the artichokes in the water and cover the dish with cling film. Cook for 10 minutes.
4. Rearrange the artichokes, so the front ones are at the back, and cook, covered, for a further 10 minutes, or until the bases are tender when pricked with a fork.
5. Leave to stand, covered, for 10 minutes. Drain off the water and leave to cool.
6. While the artichokes are cooling, make the dressing. Place the salt, pepper and mustard in a small basin. Stir in the vinegar. Whisk in the oil a little at a time, until smooth.
7. To serve, pour a little French dressing over each artichoke. Hand the remaining dressing separately.

MUSHROOMS IN GARLIC BUTTER

Preparation time: about 7 minutes Cooking time: about 8½ minutes
Microwave setting: Maximum (Full)

450 g (1 lb) button
  mushrooms
1 teaspoon dried mixed
  herbs
2 garlic cloves, peeled and
  crushed
1 tablespoon lemon juice

100 g (4 oz) butter, cut into
  pieces
1 tablespoon double cream
salt
freshly ground black
  pepper

1. Place the mushrooms, herbs, garlic and lemon juice in a large bowl. Cover and cook for 6 minutes. Pour off any excess liquid.
2. Stir in the butter, cream and salt and pepper to taste. Cook, uncovered, for 2½ minutes, stirring every minute. Serve with crusty French bread.

HOT CRAB

Preparation time: about 10 minutes Cooking time: about 3 minutes
Microwave setting: Maximum (Full)

50 g (2 oz) fresh white
    breadcrumbs
2 teaspoons oil
1 tablespoon anchovy
    essence
1 tablespoon lemon juice
1 tablespoon
    Worcestershire sauce
150 ml (¼ pint) double
    cream

175 g (6 oz) crab meat
salt
freshly ground black
    pepper
4 pieces fried bread

To garnish:
mild paprika
parsley sprigs

Frozen crab meat, thawed and drained, may be
used.
1. Place the breadcrumbs, oil, anchovy essence,
lemon juice, Worcestershire sauce, cream, crab
meat, salt and pepper in a bowl and mix them all
together.
2. Cook for 3 minutes, stirring every minute. Taste
and adjust the seasoning.
3. Spoon on to the fried bread and serve garnished
with paprika and a sprig of parsley.

ROLLMOPS

Preparation time: about 5 minutes, plus cooling
Cooking time: about 9 minutes Microwave setting: Maximum (Full)

4 medium herrings, filleted
1 large onion, peeled and
    finely sliced
300 ml (½ pint) cider
    vinegar
1 teaspoon caster sugar
salt

freshly ground black
    pepper
1 teaspoon mixed spice
2 teaspoons pickling spice
4 bay leaves

1. Roll up each herring fillet with the skin to the
outside and place in a shallow dish. Scatter the onion
over the top of the herrings.
2. Mix together the vinegar, sugar, salt, pepper,
mixed spice, pickling spice and bay leaves. Pour
the mixture over the herrings and onion.
3. Cover and cook for 5 minutes. Turn the plate
round and cook for a further 4 minutes.
4. Leave to cool before serving.

COQUILLES ST JACQUES

Preparation time: about 17 minutes Cooking time: about 15 minutes
Microwave setting: Maximum (Full)

450 g (1 lb) potatoes,
    peeled and roughly
    diced into 2.5 cm (1 inch)
    cubes
3 tablespoons water
salt
100 g (4 oz) button
    mushrooms, sliced
1 garlic clove, peeled and
    crushed
50 g (2 oz) butter
25 g (1 oz) plain flour
150 ml (¼ pint) dry white
    wine

1 egg yolk
4 large scallops, sliced,
    with shells
2 tablespoons double
    cream
freshly ground black
    pepper
1 tablespoon milk

To garnish:
4 parsley sprigs
1 scallop, sliced

1. Place the potatoes in a medium bowl with the
water and a pinch of salt. Cover and cook for 8
minutes, stirring halfway through cooking. Leave to
stand, covered, while making the sauce.
2. Place the mushrooms, garlic and 25 g (1 oz) of the
butter in a medium bowl. Cover, cook for 3 minutes.
3. Stir in the flour and wine. Cook, uncovered, for
2 minutes.
4. Beat in the egg yolk, then stir in the scallops,
cream and salt and pepper to taste. Cook,
uncovered, for 2 minutes.
5. Meanwhile, mash the potatoes with the remaining
butter, the milk and salt and pepper to taste. Place in
a piping bag filled with a large star nozzle and pipe
around the edges of 4 scallop shells.
6. Spoon the sauce into the centre. Reheat if necessary.
Serve garnished with parsley and scallop.

HOT SEAFOOD COCKTAIL

Preparation time: about 5 minutes Cooking time: 10 minutes
Microwave setting: Maximum (Full)

50 g (2 oz) butter
50 g (2 oz) plain flour
600 ml (1 pint) milk
salt
freshly ground black
    pepper
1 teaspoon tomato purée
75 g (3 oz) cooked cockles

75 g (3 oz) cooked mussels
75 g (3 oz) cooked, peeled
    prawns

To garnish:
mild paprika
whole cooked prawns
4 lemon slices

1. Place the butter in a bowl and cook for 1½ minutes.
2. Stir in the flour, then gradually blend in the milk.
Stir in the salt and pepper. Cook for 4 minutes,
stirring every minute. Taste and adjust the
seasoning.
3. Add the tomato purée to colour the sauce pink.
Stir in the cockles, mussels and prawns. Cook for 4½
minutes, stirring halfway through cooking.
4. Place the mixture in a large dish. Garnish with a
sprinkling of paprika, whole prawns and lemon
slices. Serve immediately.

From left to right clockwise:
Coquilles St Jacques; Hot seafood
cocktail; Rollmops; Hot crab

RATATOUILLE

Preparation time: about 15 minutes, plus cooling
Cooking time: about 15 minutes Microwave setting: Maximum (Full)

1 small courgette, sliced	1 tablespoon tomato purée
1 medium aubergine, sliced	2 garlic cloves, peeled and crushed
6 tomatoes, skinned and chopped	6 tablespoons olive oil
½ green pepper, cored, seeded and finely sliced	1 teaspoon dried mixed herbs
½ red pepper, cored, seeded and finely sliced	salt
1 medium onion, peeled and sliced	freshly ground black pepper

1. Place the courgette, aubergine, tomatoes, green and red peppers, onion, tomato purée, garlic, oil, herbs, salt and pepper in a large bowl. Cover and cook for 5 minutes.
2. Stir, then cook for 5 minutes. Stir again and cook for a further 5 minutes.
3. Taste and adjust the seasoning, then allow to cool before serving.

HONEYED GRAPEFRUIT & ORANGE

Preparation time: about 15 minutes Cooking time: about 3½ minutes
Microwave setting: Maximum (Full)

2 large grapefruit, halved, segmented, drained, with shells reserved	1 tablespoon clear honey
	1 tablespoon multicoloured sugar crystals or demerara sugar
1 large orange, pith and skin removed, segmented and drained	

1. Place the grapefruit and orange segments in a bowl. Add the honey. Cook for 1½ minutes.
2. Divide the mixture between the grapefruit shells. Sprinkle the sugar over each.
3. Stand the halves on a plate or in individual dishes. Cook for 2 minutes.

From left to right: Ratatouille;
Honeyed grapefruit and orange;
Jellied ham and chicken; Corn-
on-the-cob with parsley butter

JELLIED HAM & CHICKEN

Preparation time: about 8 minutes
Cooking time: about 2½ minutes, plus setting
Microwave setting: Maximum (Full)

100 g (4 oz) cooked chicken
    meat, finely diced
100 g (4 oz) cooked ham,
    finely chopped
15 g (½ oz) powdered
    gelatine
450 ml (¾ pint) well-
    flavoured chicken stock

½ teaspoon meat extract
2 teaspoons chopped fresh
    parsley
freshly ground black
    pepper
4 cucumber slices, to
    garnish

1. Mix together the chicken and ham and divide between 4 pots.
2. Place the gelatine in a jug and slowly stir in half the stock. Cook for 2½ minutes or until the gelatine has dissolved, stirring after each minute.
3. Stir in the meat extract, parsley and remaining chicken stock. Season to taste with pepper. Cool, then pour over the chicken and ham. Chill until set.
4. Garnish each pot with a slice of cucumber.

CORN-ON-THE-COB WITH PARSLEY BUTTER

Preparation time: about 5 minutes. Cooking time: about 14 minutes
Microwave setting: Maximum (Full)

75 g (3 oz) butter
4 corn-on-the-cob, fresh or
    frozen

2 tablespoons finely
    chopped fresh parsley

1. Cut the butter into pieces and place in a small dish. Heat for 1½ minutes or until melted.
2. Brush the corn with melted butter and wrap each one in greaseproof paper.
3. Arrange the corn in a shallow container. Cover and cook for 10 minutes, if fresh or 12 minutes, if frozen, until the corn is tender when pricked with a fork or skewer.
4. Remove the corn from the greaseproof paper and put into individual dishes.
5. Stir the parsley into the remaining butter and reheat for 45 seconds. Pour the hot parsley butter over the corn.

SCAMPI IN BRANDY SAUCE

Preparation time: about 8 minutes Cooking time: about 12 minutes
Microwave setting: Maximum (Full)

2 garlic cloves, peeled and
  crushed
1 medium onion, peeled
  and finely chopped
25 g (1 oz) butter
25 g (1 oz) cornflour
scant 300 ml (½ pint) milk
2 teaspoons tomato purée
2 tablespoons brandy
1 tablespoon double cream

450 g (1 lb) peeled scampi
salt
freshly ground black
  pepper

To garnish:
1 tablespoon chopped
  fresh parsley
lemon wedges

1. Place the garlic, onion and butter in a large bowl.
Cover and cook for 4 minutes.
2. Stir in the cornflour, then blend in the milk, tomato
purée, brandy, cream and scampi. Season to taste
with salt and pepper. Cook, uncovered, for 8
minutes, stirring halfway through cooking.
3. Sprinkle with parsley and serve with lemon.

PRAWNS WITH GARLIC & TOMATOES

Preparation time: about 20 minutes Cooking time: about 7 minutes
Microwave setting: Maximum (Full)

25 g (1 oz) butter
½ onion, peeled and grated
225 g (8 oz) cooked, peeled
  prawns
4 tomatoes, skinned and
  finely chopped
2 garlic cloves, peeled and
  crushed

1 tablespoon tomato purée
½ teaspoon ground mace
salt
freshly ground black
  pepper

1. Place the butter and onion in a large bowl, cover
and cook for 2 minutes.
2. Stir in the prawns, tomatoes, garlic, tomato purée,
mace, salt and pepper. Cover and cook for 5
minutes, stirring halfway through cooking.
3. Taste and adjust the seasoning.

Scampi in brandy sauce; Prawns
with garlic and tomatoes

PRAWN & LEMON PANCAKES

Preparation time: about 25 minutes, including pancakes
Cooking time: about 6 minutes Microwave setting: Maximum (Full)

1 egg (sizes 1, 2)
1 egg yolk
300 ml (½ pint) milk
pinch of salt
100 g (4 oz) plain flour
oil, for frying

300 ml (½ pint) milk
salt
freshly ground black
 pepper
1 teaspoon anchovy
 essence
grated rind of 1 small
 lemon
175 g (6 oz) cooked, peeled
 prawns

Filling:
40 g (1½ oz) butter
40 g (1½ oz) plain flour

1. Beat together the egg, egg yolk and milk. Place
the salt and flour into a mixing bowl and whisk in the
egg mixture.
2. **Make 8 pancakes using the conventional hob.** Set
aside and keep warm while making the filling.
3. Place the butter in a bowl. Cook for 45 seconds or
until melted.
4. Stir in the flour. Gradually blend in the milk and
add salt and pepper. Cook for 2½ minutes, stirring
every minute.
5. Add the anchovy essence. Taste and adjust the
seasoning. Stir in the lemon rind and prawns.
6. Spread the mixture in a line down the centre of
each pancake. Fold each edge of the pancake over
the mixture.
7. Divide the pancakes between 2 plates. Cook each
plate of pancakes for 1½ minutes.

TOMATO PASTA BOWS

Preparation time: about 10 minutes, plus standing
Cooking time: about 14 minutes Microwave setting: Maximum (Full)

1.8 litres (3 pints) boiling
 water
1 tablespoon oil
salt
225 g (8 oz) pasta bows

Sauce:
1 medium onion, peeled
 and finely chopped
2 garlic cloves, peeled and
 crushed
1 teaspoon cornflour

1 × 225 g (8 oz) can
 tomatoes, chopped with
 their juice
1 teaspoon dried mixed
 herbs
2 tablespoons tomato
 purée
salt
freshly ground black
 pepper
15 g (½ oz) butter
2 tablespoons grated
 Parmesan cheese

1. Place the boiling water, oil, salt and pasta in a
large bowl. Cover and cook for 8 minutes. Leave to
stand, covered, for 10 minutes.
2. Place the onion and garlic in a small bowl, cover
and cook for 3 minutes.
3. Stir in the cornflour, undrained tomatoes, herbs,
tomato purée and salt and pepper to taste. Cook,
uncovered, for 3 minutes, stirring halfway through.
4. Drain the pasta and stir in the sauce and butter.
Serve sprinkled with Parmesan cheese.

Prawn and lemon pancakes;
Tomato pasta bows

LIVER PÂTÉ

Preparation time: about 10 minutes, plus chilling
Cooking time: about 6½ minutes Microwave setting: Maximum (Full)

2 bacon rashers, rinds removed and chopped	1 tablespoon dried mixed herbs
225 g (8 oz) chicken livers	freshly ground black pepper
1 garlic clove, peeled and crushed	1 tablespoon dry sherry
150 g (5 oz) butter	1 tablespoon cream

1. Place the bacon in a medium bowl. Cook for 1 minute.
2. Add the livers, garlic, 100g (4 oz) of the butter, herbs and pepper. Cover and cook for 5 minutes, stirring halfway through cooking.
3. Add the sherry and cream. Place the mixture in a liquidizer and blend until smooth. Divide the pâté between 4 ramekin dishes or 1 large dish.
4. Place the remaining butter in a bowl. Cook for 30 seconds or until melted. Pour a little butter over each serving of the pâté.
5. Allow to cool completely, then chill for 2 hours.

KIPPER PÂTÉ

Preparation time: about 10 minutes, plus chilling
Cooking time: about 9 minutes Microwave setting: Maximum (Full)

225 g (8 oz) frozen kipper fillets	¼ teaspoon ground mace
1 small onion, peeled and chopped	1 tablespoon lemon juice
50 g (2 oz) butter	salt
75 g (3 oz) full fat soft cheese	freshly ground black pepper
	parsley sprigs, to garnish

1. Place the kippers in a shallow dish. Cover and cook for 2½ minutes.
2. Separate the fillets. Cook for a further 2½ minutes. Set aside.
3. Place the onion and butter in a bowl, cover and cook for 4 minutes.
4. Chop the kippers and add to the onion and butter. Stir in the cheese, mace, lemon juice, salt and pepper.
5. Place the mixture in a liquidizer and blend.
6. Divide the pâté between 4 ramekin dishes. Allow to cool completely and chill for 2 hours. Garnish with parsley sprigs.

Liver pâté; Kipper pâté

STUFFED TOMATOES

Preparation time: about 10 minutes Cooking time: about 5½ minutes
Microwave setting: Maximum (Full)

4 large tomatoes, about 750 g (1½ lb)
40 g (1½ oz) fresh brown breadcrumbs
15 g (½ oz) Cheddar cheese, finely grated
25 g (1 oz) chopped ham
1 teaspoon mixed dried herbs

1 teaspoon made English mustard
2 tablespoons plain unsweetened yogurt
salt
freshly ground black pepper
4 parsley sprigs, to garnish

1. Slice the top off each of the tomatoes and reserve, then, using a grapefruit knife, scoop out the centres. Chop the flesh and seeds, then mix with the breadcrumbs, cheese, ham, herbs, mustard, yogurt and salt and pepper to taste.
2. Fill each tomato with the stuffing and replace the 'lids' on top of the tomatoes.
3. Place the tomatoes in 4 small dishes and arrange in a circle in the cooker. Cook, uncovered, for 5½ minutes or until soft, rearranging halfway through cooking. Remove any which may be cooked before the total cooking time.
4. Garnish each tomato with a sprig of parsley.

STUFFED BAKED AVOCADO WITH SHRIMPS

Preparation time: about 10 minutes Cooking time: about 5 minutes
Microwave setting: Maximum (Full)

25 g (1 oz) butter
50 g (2 oz) fresh brown breadcrumbs
1 tablespoon grated lemon rind
100 g (4 oz) peeled shrimps
5 tablespoons single cream
salt

freshly ground black pepper
2 large ripe avocados
1 tablespoon lemon juice

To garnish:
lettuce leaves
lemon twists

1. Place the butter in a bowl. Cook for 30 seconds or until melted.
2. Stir in the breadcrumbs. Cook for 1 minute. Stir in lemon rind, shrimps, cream, salt and pepper.
3. Cut the avocados in half. Remove and discard the stones, then sprinkle the flesh with lemon juice.
4. Pile the shrimp mixture into each of the avocado halves. Arrange on a plate. Cook for 3½ minutes.
5. Serve on lettuce garnished with lemon.

Stuffed tomatoes: Stuffed baked avocado with shrimps

EGGS, CHEESE & CREAM

CURRIED EGGS

Preparation time: about 8 minutes Cooking time: about 8 minutes
Microwave setting: Maximum (Full)

4 eggs
1 medium onion, peeled
  and finely chopped
1 garlic clove, peeled and
  crushed
1 tablespoon tomato purée
1 tablespoon lemon juice
1 tablespoon medium
  curry powder

1 teaspoon mild chilli
  powder
2 tablespoons white wine
  vinegar
15 g ($\frac{1}{2}$ oz) butter
15 g ($\frac{1}{2}$ oz) flour
300 ml ($\frac{1}{2}$ pint) hot chicken
  stock
4 lemon slices, to garnish

1. Place the eggs in a saucepan and cover with water. Bring to the boil and **cook the eggs conventionally on the hob** for 8 minutes to hard-boil.
2. Meanwhile, place the onion, garlic, tomato purée, lemon juice, curry powder, chilli powder and vinegar in a medium bowl. Cover and cook for 5 minutes, stirring halfway through cooking.
3. Stir in the butter until melted. Stir in the flour and blend in the stock. Cook, uncovered, for 3 minutes, stirring every minute.
4. Plunge the eggs into cold water and remove the shells. Cut each egg in half and arrange, cut sides down, on a serving dish. Strain the sauce and pour over eggs. Garnish with lemon slices.
5. Serve with boiled rice, sliced tomatoes and desiccated coconut.

Curried eggs

FRIED EGGS

Preparation time: about 2 minutes
Cooking time: about 1¾ minutes, plus standing
Microwave setting: Maximum (Full)

Serves 2

20 g (¾ oz) butter
2 eggs (size 3), taken from
  refrigerator

freshly ground black
  pepper (optional)

1. Divide the butter between two 12.5 cm (5 inch) top diameter saucers. Cook for 30 seconds or until melted.
2. Break an egg into each saucer and pierce the yolk with a cocktail stick. Sprinkle with pepper, if desired. Cover tightly with cling film.
3. Cook for 1¼ minutes, turning round halfway through cooking. Leave to stand, covered, for 1 minute before serving. If the egg is not cooked, return to the cooker for 15 seconds.

BAKED EGGS

Preparation time: about 5 minutes Cooking time: about 4½ minutes
Microwave setting: Maximum (Full)

15 g (½ oz) butter
2 small mushrooms, finely
  chopped
50 g (2 oz) ham, finely
  chopped
4 teaspoons tomato purée

4 eggs (sizes 1, 2)
salt
freshly ground black
  pepper
4 tablespoons double
  cream

1. Divide the butter and mushrooms between the bases of 4 cocotte dishes. Cook for 1½ minutes.
2. Place the ham on the mushrooms and 1 teaspoon of the tomato purée on the ham in each dish.
3. Break the eggs on to the ham and pierce the yolks with a needle. Season with salt and pepper.
4. Pour 1 tablespoon cream over each of the eggs. Cook for 1½ minutes.
5. Rearrange the dishes, so the front ones are at the back, and cook for a further 1½ minutes. Serve the eggs at once.

From left to right: Fried eggs;
Baked eggs; Omelette; Poached
eggs

OMELETTE

Preparation time: about 3 minutes Cooking time: 3¾ minutes
Microwave setting: Maximum (Full)

Serves 2

4 eggs (size 2)
4 tablespoons milk
salt
freshly ground black
   pepper

20 g (¾ oz) butter
1 tablespoon chopped
   fresh parsley, to garnish

1. Beat together the eggs, milk and salt and pepper
to taste.
2. Place the butter in a 23 cm (9 inch) round shallow
casserole. Cook, uncovered, for 30 seconds.
3. Tilt the casserole to be sure the bottom is evenly
coated with melted butter, then pour in the egg
mixture. Cover and cook for 2 minutes.
4. Using a fork, draw the edges of the egg to the
centre. Cover and cook for a further 1¼ minutes. If
not quite cooked, stand for 1 minute before serving.
5. Serve sprinkled with chopped parsley.

Variation:
Chopped ham could be added at step 4 after the
cooking is completed.

POACHED EGGS

Preparation time: about 2 minutes
Cooking time: about 3 minutes, plus standing
Microwave setting: Maximum (Full)

Serves 2

125 ml (4 fl oz) water
2 tablespoons white
   vinegar

2 eggs (size 2)
hot buttered toast, to serve

1. Divide the water and vinegar equally between 2
ramekin dishes. Cook, uncovered, for 2 minutes or
until boiling.
2. Break the eggs into the water and cook,
uncovered, for 1 minute.
3. Leave the eggs to stand for 1 minute.
4. Drain off the water and vinegar, then serve on hot
buttered toast.

BOILED EGGS

Eggs must **never** be cooked in their shells in a
microwave cooker as there is a build-up of pressure
within the egg which causes the shell to 'explode' or
burst. As a result, the cooker interior would have to
be cleaned which is a nuisance, but more important,
the impact could cause damage to the components
of the cooker. Piercing the shell does not prevent it.

EGGS BENEDICT

Preparation time: about 10 minutes Cooking time: about 4½ minutes
Microwave setting: Maximum (Full)

4 slices of cooked ham
4 thick slices of buttered
   white toast, cut to the size
   of the ham

Poached eggs:
250 ml (8 fl oz) water
4 tablespoons white
   vinegar

4 eggs (size 3)

Hollandaise sauce:
2 egg yolks (size 3)
1 tablespoon lemon juice
100 g (4 oz) butter, cut into
   8 pieces
pinch of cayenne pepper
½ teaspoon dry mustard

1. Place a piece of ham on each slice of toast. Keep warm.
2. Divide the water and vinegar equally between 4 ramekin dishes. Cook, uncovered, for 2 minutes or until boiling. Break an egg into each dish.
3. To make the sauce, prick the egg yolks and place with the lemon juice in a small bowl. Cook, uncovered, for 30 seconds. Beat hard until smooth.
4. Place the eggs for poaching into the cooker and cook for 2 minutes. Stand for 1 minute before draining.
5. Meanwhile, beat a piece of butter at a time into the sauce, until all 8 pieces are incorporated. Beat in the cayenne pepper and mustard.
6. Place the poached eggs on the ham and toast and top with a large spoon of sauce. Serve at once.

EGGS FLORENTINE

Preparation time: about 4 minutes
Cooking time: about 3¾ minutes, plus standing
Microwave setting: Maximum (Full)

1 × 225 g (8 oz) can
   chopped spinach,
   drained or frozen
   spinach, thawed and
   drained
salt

freshly ground black
   pepper
¼ teaspoon grated nutmeg
4 eggs (size 2), from
   refrigerator

1. Divide the spinach between 4 ramekin dishes. Cook, uncovered, for 1½ minutes.
2. Sprinkle the spinach with a little salt, pepper and nutmeg. Break the eggs on to the spinach. Prick the yolks and cover dishes with cling film. Arrange in a circle in the cooker.
3. Cook for 2¼ minutes, rearranging the dishes halfway through cooking. If the eggs are not quite cooked, allow to stand, covered, for 1 minute.
4. Serve with hot buttered toast.

Eggs benedict; Eggs Florentine

WELSH RAREBIT

Preparation time: about 5 minutes
Cooking time: about 1½ minutes plus grilling
Microwave setting: Maximum (Full)

225 g (8 oz) Cheddar
   cheese, finely grated
4 tablespoons milk
salt
freshly ground black
   pepper

1 teaspoon French mustard
4 slices toast
parsley sprigs, to garnish

1. Place the cheese and milk in a medium bowl and cook for 1 minute.
2. Stir in the salt, pepper and mustard and cook for 30 seconds.
3. Spread the cheese mixture over the toast and garnish with the chopped parsley.
4. If desired, **place the Welsh rarebit under a preheated conventional grill**, to brown the top, before garnishing with parsley.

CHEESE & HAM PUDDING

Preparation time: about 10 minutes, plus standing
Cooking time: about 10–12 minutes
Microwave setting: Maximum (Full)

225 g (8 oz) fresh brown
   breadcrumbs
50 g (2 oz) cooked ham,
   finely chopped
pinch of dry mustard
1 teaspoon dried mixed
   herbs
175 g (6 oz) mild Cheddar
   cheese, finely grated

salt
freshly ground black
   pepper
3 eggs, lightly beaten
600 ml (1 pint) milk
1 tablespoon chopped
   fresh parsley, to garnish

1. Mix together the breadcrumbs, ham, mustard, herbs, cheese and salt and pepper to taste. Lightly beat in the eggs and milk. Pour into a 1.75 litre (3 pint) soufflé dish. Allow to stand for 10 minutes.
2. Cook, uncovered, for 10–12 minutes, stirring halfway through cooking.
3. Sprinkle with parsley and serve with a green vegetable.

Welsh rarebit; Cheese and ham
pudding

SALAMI & CHEESE FLAN

Preparation time: about 15 minutes
Cooking time: about 13½ minutes, plus grilling
Microwave setting: Maximum (Full)

175 g (6 oz) prepared
  shortcrust pastry
125 ml (4 fl oz) milk
3 eggs
75 g (3 oz) salami, finely
  diced
salt

freshly ground black
  pepper
50 g (2 oz) Samsoe or
  Cheddar cheese, finely
  grated
parsley sprig, to garnish

The results of this flan may not be quite the same as if cooked by the conventional method. However; the flavour is excellent and it is a speedy dish to make. The egg mixture will still be wet in the centre after microwave cooking, but it sets during grilling.
1. Roll out the pastry and line a 17 cm (6½ inch) base diameter, 22 cm (8½ inch) top diameter plate tart dish. Prick the sides and base with a fork. Cook for 3½ minutes or until the pastry looks dry. Set aside.
2. Place the milk, eggs, salami, salt and pepper in a jug. Lightly beat together. Cook for 2 minutes, beating with a fork every ½ minute.
3. Pour the mixture into the pastry case and cook for 3 minutes, stirring gently after 1 and 2 minutes.
4. Sprinkle the cheese over the egg and **brown under a preheated conventional grill** for about 5 minutes. Serve garnished with a sprig of parsley.

SMOKED HADDOCK WITH EGG SAUCE

Preparation time: about 10 minutes, plus infusing
Cooking time: about 11 minutes Microwave setting: Maximum (Full)

300 ml (½ pint) milk
1 bay leaf
1 onion slice
8 smoked haddock fillets
50 g (2 oz) butter
25 g (1 oz) plain flour
salt

freshly ground black
  pepper
2 hard-boiled eggs, finely
  chopped
2 tablespoons chopped
  fresh chives

1. Place the milk in a jug with the bay leaf and onion slice and cook for 2 minutes. Leave for 15 minutes.
2. Place the haddock fillets in a shallow dish and dot with 25 g (1 oz) of the butter. Cover and cook for 2 minutes. Turn the dish round and cook for a further 2 minutes. Keep warm while making the sauce.
3. Place the remaining butter in a 600 ml (1 pint) jug. Cook for 1 minute or until melted. Blend in the flour.
4. Strain the hot milk, discarding the bay leaf and onion, and stir it into the roux. Add salt and pepper. Cook for 2 minutes, stirring every minute.
5. Stir in the chopped hard-boiled eggs and chives.
6. Pour the sauce over the fish and reheat for 2 minutes before serving.

Salami and cheese flan; Smoked
haddock with egg sauce

BREAKFAST FOR TWO

2 slices of toast, halved (optional)
Kidneys, mushrooms and bacon
Scrambled eggs

Order of cooking

1. Toast the bread in the conventional manner. Cook the kidneys, mushrooms and bacon as directed. Cover and keep hot.
2. Make the scrambled eggs.
3. Warm the toast (if using) for 30 seconds on a piece of kitchen towel, and serve.

SCRAMBLED EGGS

Preparation time: about 2 minutes
Cooking time: about 3 minutes, plus making toast
Microwave setting: Maximum (Full)

Serves 2

4 eggs (size 2)	15 g ($\frac{1}{2}$ oz) butter
1 tablespoon milk	hot buttered toast, to serve
salt	2 parsley sprigs, to garnish
freshly ground black pepper	(optional)

1. Place the eggs, milk, salt and pepper to taste in a large jug and beat well. Add the butter.
2. Cook, uncovered, for 3 minutes or until the desired consistency is reached. Break up the mixture and beat gently after every minute.
3. Serve on hot buttered toast garnished with parsley (if using).

KIDNEYS, MUSHROOMS & BACON

Preparation time: about 3 minutes Cooking time: about 5$\frac{1}{2}$ minutes
Microwave setting: Maximum (Full)

Serves 2

4 rashers streaky bacon, rinds removed	2 lambs' kidneys, membrane and core removed and halved
	4 flat mushrooms

1. Place a piece of absorbent paper towel on a plate. Place the bacon on one side, cover with another piece of paper and cook for 1 minute.
2. Uncover. Place the mushrooms in the centre of the plate, cover and cook for 1$\frac{1}{2}$ minutes, then put the kidneys round the outside of the plate, recover, and cook for 2 minutes, turning the kidneys over and rearranging the mushrooms if necessary. Re-cover and cook for 1 minute.
3. Serve at once. Or, if being served with scrambled egg, remove the paper towels and cover with a plate to keep hot while cooking the eggs.

Scrambled eggs; Kidneys,
mushrooms and bacon

BEEF

BEEF TOURNEDOS WITH PÂTÉ

Preparation time: about 20 minutes   Cooking time: about 12–14 minutes
Microwave setting: Maximum (Full)

1 medium onion, peeled
  and chopped
50 g (2 oz) button
  mushrooms, peeled and
  sliced
1 garlic clove, peeled and
  crushed
$\frac{1}{2}$ teaspoon dried tarragon
$\frac{1}{4}$ teaspoon dried oregano
1 teaspoon dried rosemary
25 g (1 oz) butter, cut into
  pieces
25 g (1 oz) plain flour
3 tablespoons tomato
  purée

300 ml ($\frac{1}{2}$ pint) hot beef
  stock
salt
freshly ground black
  pepper
4 fillet steaks, 2.5 cm
  (1 inch) thick, 7.5–10 cm
  (3–4 inches) wide, total
  weight 600 g ($1\frac{1}{4}$ lb)
4 slices fried bread, 5 mm
  ($\frac{1}{4}$ inch) thick
225 g (8 oz) chicken liver
  pâté

1. Place the onion, mushrooms, garlic, tarragon,
oregano and rosemary in a large jug. Cover and
cook for 3 minutes.
2. Stir in the butter until melted. Stir in the flour.
Blend in the tomato purée, stock, and salt and
pepper to taste. Cook uncovered for 3 minutes,
stirring every minute. Set aside, covered.
3. Place the steaks in a shallow 1.5 litre ($2\frac{1}{2}$ pint)
casserole dish. Cook, uncovered, for 3–5 minutes,
depending on how rare you like your steak, and
turning over and rearranging halfway through
cooking. Pour the steak juices into the sauce.
4. Cut the fried bread to fit the steaks. Spread each
piece of bread with pâté. Place steak on the top.
Cook, uncovered, for 3 minutes.
5. Pour over the sauce and serve, with a mixed
green salad.

GARLIC ROAST BEEF

Preparation time: about 10 minutes
Cooking time: about 20 minutes, plus standing and grilling
Microwave setting: Maximum (Full)

1.5 kg (3 lb) topside of beef	salt
oil, to coat	freshly ground black
3 garlic cloves, peeled	pepper

1. Rub the beef with the oil, 1 of the garlic cloves, and salt and pepper.
2. Stand the beef on an upturned saucer in a shallow container and cook for 10 minutes.
3. With a sharp knife, cut the remaining garlic cloves into slivers. Make incisions in the meat and insert the slivers of garlic.
4. Cook for 10 minutes.
5. Remove the meat and wrap tightly in foil, with the shiny side inside. Leave the meat to stand for 20 minutes. **Brown under a preheated conventional grill** then carve.

Garlic roast beef; Beef olives

BEEF OLIVES

Preparation time: about 20 minutes Cooking time: about 13 minutes
Microwave setting: Maximum (Full)

50 g (2 oz) mushrooms	450 g (1 lb) topside of beef,
1 onion, peeled and	cut into 4 thin slices and
quartered	lightly beaten
1 tablespoon orange juice	$\frac{1}{2}$ green pepper, cored,
3 tablespoons beef stock	seeded and chopped
grated rind of 1 lemon	100 g (4 oz) mushrooms,
$\frac{1}{2}$ teaspoon dried mixed	chopped
herbs	40 g (1$\frac{1}{2}$ oz) butter, diced
salt	2 tablespoons plain flour
freshly ground pepper	150 ml ($\frac{1}{4}$ pint) white wine
25 g (1 oz) fresh white	1 teaspoon soy sauce
breadcrumbs	chopped parsley, to
	garnish

1. Purée the whole mushrooms, onion, orange juice, stock, lemon rind, herbs and salt and pepper to taste. Stir in the breadcrumbs.
2. Divide the mixture between the slices of beef and roll up. Secure. Cook, uncovered for 6 minutes, turning over halfway through. Set aside, covered.
3. Place the green pepper and chopped mushrooms in a large jug. Cover and cook for 4 minutes. Stir in the butter until melted. Stir in the flour, wine, soy sauce and meat juices. Season. Pour over the beef. Cook for 3 minutes. Garnish with parsley.

TARRAGON BEEF

Preparation time: about 6 minutes Cooking time: about 10 minutes
Microwave setting: Maximum (Full)

3 tablespoons fresh
  tarragon
4 fillet steaks, total weight
  750 g (1½ lb), lightly
  beaten
25 g (1 oz) butter
about 150 ml (¼ pint) hot
  beef stock
15 g (½ oz) cornflour

salt
freshly ground black
  pepper
6 tablespoons double
  cream
fresh tarragon, to garnish

1. Sprinkle 2 tablespoons of the tarragon over both
sides of the steaks and rub in well. Place the steaks
in a shallow dish and cook, uncovered, for 7
minutes, turning over and rearranging halfway
through cooking. Pour off and reserve the juices.

2. Place the butter in a large jug and cook,
uncovered, for 30 seconds or until melted. Make up
the meat juices to 150 ml (¼ pint) with the stock, then
stir in with the cornflour, remaining tarragon, and
salt and pepper to taste. Cook, uncovered, for 2½
minutes, stirring every minute.
3. Stir in the cream and pour over the steaks and
reheat for 1 minute if necessary. Garnish with
tarragon and serve with a mixed green salad.

Tarragon beef

BEEF IN BEER

Preparation time: about 21 minutes
Cooking time: about 53 minutes, plus standing
Microwave setting: Maximum (Full) and Defrost

l medium onion, peeled
  and sliced
175 g (6 oz) carrots, peeled
  and sliced
l celery stick, chopped
600 g (1¼ lb) topside beef,
  cut into cubes
25 g (1 oz) butter, diced
25 g (1 oz) plain flour

l tablespoon tomato purée
l teaspoon dried mixed
  herbs
150 ml (¼ pint) brown ale
300 ml (½ pint) hot beef
  stock
salt
freshly ground black
  pepper

1. Place the onion, carrots and celery in a large
bowl. Cover and cook on Maximum for 5 minutes,
stirring halfway through cooking.
2. Stir in the beef and butter, cover and cook on
Maximum for 3 minutes. Stir in the flour, tomato
purée, herbs, ale, stock, and salt and pepper to
taste. Cover and cook for 5 minutes.
3. Cook, uncovered, for a further 40 minutes on
Defrost, stirring several times during cooking.
4. Stand, covered, for 10 minutes before serving.
Serve with boiled noodles.

BEEF IN CIDER

Preparation time: about 15 minutes
Cooking time: 52 minutes, plus standing
Microwave setting: Maximum (Full) and Defrost

½ green pepper, cored,
  seeded and finely
  chopped
2 medium onions, peeled
  and thinly sliced
l kg (2 lb) silverside beef,
  trimmed and cubed
40 g (1½ oz) butter, cut into
  pieces
50 g (2 oz) plain flour

l bay leaf
½ teaspoon dried oregano
½ teaspoon dried thyme
l tablespoon tomato purée
300 ml (½ pint) dry cider
150 ml (¼ pint) hot beef
  stock
salt
freshly ground black
  pepper

1. Place the green pepper and onions in a large
bowl, cover and cook on Maximum for 5 minutes.
2. Stir in the beef and butter. Cover and cook on
Maximum for 7 minutes, stirring twice.
3. Stir in the flour, bay leaf, oregano, thyme, tomato
purée, cider, stock and salt and pepper to taste.
Cover and cook on Defrost for 40 minutes, stirring
twice during cooking. Leave to stand, covered, for
10 minutes.
4. Discard the bay leaf, then taste and adjust the
seasoning.

BEEF GOULASH

Preparation time: about 15 minutes
Cooking time: about 49 minutes, plus standing
Microwave setting: Maximum (Full) and Defrost

1 large onion, peeled and
 sliced
25 g (1 oz) butter
125 ml (4 fl oz) tomato
 purée
1 tablespoon ground
 Hungarian paprika
2 teaspoons caster sugar
2 tomatoes, skinned and
 chopped
600 g (1¼ lb) topside of
 beef, cubed

salt
freshly ground black
 pepper
2 tablespoons plain flour
300 ml (½ pint) hot beef
 stock
2 tablespoons soured
 cream
paprika, to garnish

1. Place the onion in a large bowl, cover and cook on Maximum for 4 minutes. Stir in the butter, tomato purée, paprika, sugar, tomatoes, beef and salt and pepper to taste. Cook, covered, on Maximum for 5 minutes, stirring halfway through cooking.
2. Stir in the flour and stock. Cover and cook on Defrost for 40 minutes, stirring twice during cooking. Leave to stand, covered, for 10 minutes.
3. Stir in the soured cream and sprinkle with paprika. Serve with ribbon noodles.

BEEF STROGANOFF

Preparation time: about 15 minutes Cooking time: about 12 minutes
Microwave setting: Maximum (Full)

50 g (2 oz) butter
1 tablespoon tomato purée
1 large onion, peeled and
 finely diced
175 g (6 oz) mushrooms,
 sliced
750 g (1½ lb) beef fillet, cut
 into strips, 7.5 × 1 cm (3
 inches × ½ inch)

150 ml (¼ pint) dry white
 wine
25 g (1 oz) cornflour
salt
freshly ground black
 pepper
50 ml (2 fl oz) soured cream
chopped fresh parsley, to
 garnish

1. Place the butter, tomato purée, onion and mushrooms in a large bowl. Cover and cook for 5 minutes.
2. Stir in the beef, cover and cook for 5 minutes.
3. Blend together the wine and cornflour, then stir into the beef. Cook, uncovered, for 2 minutes, stirring halfway through cooking.
4. Add salt and pepper to taste, stir in the soured cream and serve on a bed of boiled rice, garnished with parsley.

Left: Beef in beer; Beef in cider.
Right: Beef goulash; Beef stroganoff

BEEF, MUSHROOM & ONION SUET PUDDING

Preparation time: about 30 minutes Cooking time: about 18 minutes
Microwave setting: Maximum (Full)

Pastry:
225 g (8 oz) self-raising
   flour
½ teaspoon salt
100 g (4 oz) shredded suet
175–200 ml (6–7 fl oz) water

Filling:
25 g (1 oz) butter
2 medium onions, peeled
   and sliced
100 g (4 oz) mushrooms,
   chopped

1 garlic clove, peeled and
   crushed
¼ teaspoon dried parsley
¼ teaspoon dried rosemary
¼ teaspoon dried oregano
¼ teaspoon dried marjoram
   salt
freshly ground black
   pepper
350 g (12 oz) minced beef
½ teaspoon meat extract
parsley sprig, to garnish

1. Mix together the flour, salt, suet and enough water to form a smooth dough. Roll out two-thirds of the pastry and use to line a greased 1.2 litre (2 pint) pudding basin. Roll out the remainder for a lid and set aside.

2. Place the butter, onions, mushrooms, garlic, parsley, rosemary, oregano, marjoram and salt and pepper to taste in a medium bowl. Cover and cook for 5 minutes.
3. Stir in the beef and meat extract. Cover and cook for 4 minutes, stirring halfway through cooking. Drain off the excess liquid.
4. Fill the basin with the mixture. Place the pastry lid in position and seal. Cover loosely with cling film and cook for 9 minutes, turning round halfway through cooking.
5. Serve immediately, garnished with the parsley and accompanied by creamed potatoes and carrots.

Above: Beef, mushroom and onion suet pudding; Right: Chilli con carne; Beef bourguignon

CHILLI CON CARNE

Preparation time: about 10 minutes Cooking time: about 17 minutes
Microwave setting: Maximum (Full)

1 large onion, peeled and
finely chopped
1 garlic clove, peeled and
crushed
2 teaspoons tomato purée
25 g (1 oz) butter, cut into
pieces
25 g (1 oz) plain flour
½ teaspoon dried oregano
½ teaspoon ground cumin

2 teaspoons chilli powder
1 × 400 g (14 oz) can
tomatoes, chopped with
their juice
450 g (1 lb) minced beef
1 × 425 g (15 oz) can red
kidney beans, drained
salt
freshly ground black
pepper

1. Place the onion, garlic and tomato purée in a large
bowl. Cover and cook for 5 minutes.
2. Stir in the butter until melted. Stir in the flour,
oregano, cumin, chilli powder, undrained tomatoes
and beef. Cook, uncovered, for 8 minutes. Stir and
break up with a fork halfway through cooking.
3. Stir in the beans and cook, uncovered, for 4
minutes, stirring halfway through cooking.
4. Season to taste with salt and pepper and serve
with boiled rice.

BEEF BOURGUIGNON

Preparation time: about 15 minutes
Cooking time: about 56 minutes, plus standing
Microwave setting: Maximum (Full) and Defrost

2 medium onions, peeled
and chopped
2 bacon rashers, rinds
removed and chopped
175 g (6 oz) mushrooms,
sliced
750 g (1½ lb) topside of
beef, cubed
25 g (1 oz) plain flour

225 ml (7½ fl oz) red wine
65 ml (2½ fl oz) hot beef
stock
2 garlic cloves, peeled and
crushed
1 teaspoon dried mixed
herbs
salt
freshly ground black
pepper

1. Place the onions and bacon in a large bowl, cover
and cook on Maximum for 5 minutes.
2. Stir in the mushrooms and beef, cover and cook
on Maximum for 7 minutes, stirring halfway through.
3. Stir in the flour, red wine, stock, garlic, herbs and
salt and pepper to taste. Cover and cook on
Maximum for 4 minutes, stirring halfway through
cooking, then reduce to Defrost and cook for 40
minutes.
4. Leave to stand, covered, for 10 minutes.

BEEF WITH CHEESE SAUCE

Preparation time: about 20 minutes
Cooking time: 22 minutes, plus grilling
Microwave setting: Maximum (Full)

1 onion, peeled and thinly
    sliced
1 medium carrot, peeled
    and sliced
100 g (4 oz) potato, peeled
    and sliced
100 g (4 oz) mushrooms,
    chopped
1 tablespoon tomato purée
350 g (12 oz) minced beef
1 teaspoon dried mixed
    herbs

salt
freshly ground black
    pepper
40 g (1½ oz) butter
40 g (1½ oz) plain flour
600 ml (1 pint) milk
100 g (4 oz) Cheddar
    cheese, finely grated
1 tablespoon chopped
    fresh parsley, to garnish

1. Place the onion, carrot and potato in a 1.5 litre (2½ pint) soufflé dish. Cover and cook for 4½ minutes, stirring halfway through cooking.
2. Stir in the mushrooms, tomato purée, beef, herbs, and salt and pepper to taste. Cover and cook for 8 minutes. Break up and stir with a fork halfway through cooking. Set aside, covered.
3. Place the butter in a large jug and cook, uncovered, for 30 seconds or until melted. Stir in the flour, then gradually blend in the milk, with salt and pepper to taste. Cook, uncovered, for 7 minutes or until thick, stirring every 2 minutes.
4. Stir in the cheese until melted. Pour the sauce over the beef mixture. Cook, uncovered, for 2 minutes. **Brown under a preheated conventional grill, if preferred.**
5. Sprinkle with parsley to garnish. Serve with sauté potatoes and peas.

Below: Beef with cheese sauce;
Right: Chinese style beef;
Mexican beef

CHINESE STYLE BEEF

Preparation time: about 15 minutes
Cooking time: about 12 minutes, plus standing
Microwave setting: Maximum (Full)

1 tablespoon sesame oil
2 medium onions, peeled and sliced
1 red pepper, cored, seeded and thinly sliced
1 garlic clove, peeled and crushed
600 g (1¼ lb) fillet steak, cut into strips, 7.5 cm × 1 cm (3 inches × ½ inch)
100 g (4 oz) button mushrooms, sliced
1 teaspoon ground ginger
¼ teaspoon ground cumin
¼ teaspoon grated nutmeg

1 teaspoon dried mixed herbs
15 g (½ oz) cornflour
1 tablespoon lemon juice
50 ml (2 fl oz) dry sherry
175 ml (6 fl oz) hot beef stock
1 tablespoon Worcestershire sauce
1 tablespoon soy sauce
salt
freshly ground black pepper
1 × 275 g (10 oz) can bean sprouts, drained

1. Place the oil, onions, red pepper and garlic in a large bowl. Cover and cook for 5 minutes, stirring halfway through cooking.
2. Stir in the beef, mushrooms, ginger, cumin, nutmeg, and herbs. Cover and cook for 3 minutes.
3. Stir in the cornflour, lemon juice, sherry, stock, Worcestershire sauce, soy sauce and salt and pepper to taste. Fold in the bean sprouts. Cover and cook for 4 minutes, stirring halfway through.
4. Leave to stand, covered, for 4 minutes before serving. Serve with boiled rice.

MEXICAN BEEF

Preparation time: about 20 minutes
Cooking time: about 15½ minutes, plus standing
Microwave setting: Maximum (Full)

1 medium onion, peeled and sliced
1 small carrot, peeled and sliced
1 green pepper, cored, seeded and chopped
1 red pepper, cored, seeded and chopped
1 medium potato, peeled and diced
50 g (2 oz) butter, cut into pieces
1 teaspoon dried mixed herbs
½ teaspoon chilli powder

½ teaspoon Worcestershire sauce
1 teaspoon dried parsley
1 garlic clove, peeled and crushed
600 g (1¼ lb) topside beef, cut into strips
salt
freshly ground black pepper
2 tablespoons plain flour
1 × 400 g (14 oz) can tomatoes, chopped with their juice
150 ml (¼ pint) hot beef stock

1. Place the onion, carrot, peppers and potato in a large bowl. Cover and cook for 6½ minutes.
2. Stir in the butter until melted. Stir in the herbs, chilli powder, Worcestershire sauce, parsley, garlic, beef, and salt and pepper to taste. Cover and cook for 4 minutes, stirring halfway through.
3. Stir in the flour, undrained tomatoes and stock. Cover and cook for 5 minutes, stirring halfway through cooking.
4. Leave to stand, covered, for 5 minutes.

STEAK WITH CHESTNUTS

Preparation time: about 15 minutes Cooking time: about 12–14 minutes
Microwave setting: Maximum (Full)

4 fillet steaks, 2.5 cm
(1 inch) thick, total
weight 450 g (1 lb),
lightly beaten
1 small celery stick,
chopped
½ green pepper, cored,
seeded and chopped
½ red pepper, cored,
seeded and chopped
1 garlic clove, peeled and
crushed

2 tablespoons tomato
purée
15 g (½ oz) cornflour
3 tablespoons dry sherry
2 tablespoons soy sauce
6 canned water chestnuts,
drained and sliced
salt
freshly ground black
pepper

1. Place the steaks in a casserole dish. Cook,
uncovered, for 3–5 minutes, depending on how rare
you like your steak, and turning over and
rearranging halfway through cooking. Set aside,
covered, while making sauce.
2. Place the celery, peppers, garlic and tomato
purée in a medium bowl. Cover and cook for 5
minutes, stirring halfway through cooking.
3. Stir in the cornflour, sherry, soy sauce, water
chestnuts, and salt and pepper to taste. Add any
juice from the cooked steaks.
4. Pour the mixture over the steaks. Cover and cook
for 4 minutes. Serve with croquette potatoes.

STEAK IN PEPPER SAUCE

Preparation time: about 10 minutes
Cooking time: about 13½ minutes, plus standing
Microwave setting: Maximum (Full)

1 medium onion, peeled
and finely chopped
50 g (2 oz) butter
1 garlic clove, peeled and
crushed
40 g (1½ oz) cornflour
300 ml (½ pint) hot beef
stock

150 ml (¼ pint) milk
½ teaspoon freshly ground
black pepper
16 whole black
peppercorns
salt
4 sirloin steaks

1. Place the onion, butter and garlic in a medium
bowl. Cover and cook for 4 minutes.
2. Stir in the cornflour, hot stock, milk and ground
pepper. Crush 6 of the peppercorns and add them
to the sauce with the remaining peppercorns and
the salt.
3. Cover and cook for 2 minutes, stirring halfway
through cooking. Leave covered and set aside.
4. Place the steaks in a large shallow casserole.
Cook for 3 minutes. Turn the steaks over and turn
the casserole round. Cook for a further 2¼ minutes.
5. Stir any meat juices into the sauce. Pour the sauce
over the steaks, cover and cook for 2 minutes.
6. Leave to stand, covered, for 3 minutes before
serving. Serve with a mixed salad.

Whisky steak; Steak with mushroom sauce

WHISKY STEAK

Preparation time: about 7 minutes, plus marinating
Cooking time: about 14 minutes Microwave setting: Maximum (Full)

4 rump steaks, total weight
  750 g (1½ lb), lightly
  beaten
2 tablespoons whisky
1 garlic clove, peeled and
  crushed
1 medium onion, peeled
  and finely chopped

50 g (2 oz) butter
½ teaspoon Worcestershire
  sauce
freshly ground black
  pepper
spring onions, to garnish

1. Marinate the steaks in the whisky for 2 hours.
2. Place the garlic and onion in a large jug. Cook,
covered, for 4 minutes. Stir in the butter and cook,
uncovered, for 30 seconds. Set aside while cooking
the steaks.
3. Drain the steaks, reserving the marinade. Place
the steaks in a shallow casserole dish. Cook,
uncovered, for 7 minutes, turning over and
rearranging halfway through cooking.
4. Pour the juice from the steaks into the butter
mixture. Stir in the Worcestershire sauce, whisky
from the marinade and pepper to taste.
5. Pour the sauce over the steaks and cook,
uncovered, for 2½ minutes.
6. Garnish with spring onions and serve with plain
boiled rice and broccoli.

STEAK WITH MUSHROOM SAUCE

Preparation time: about 15 minutes, plus infusing
Cooking time: about 20 minutes Microwave setting: Maximum (Full)

1 celery stick, chopped
1 onion, peeled and
  studded with 6 cloves
1 carrot, peeled and sliced
450 ml (¾ pint) milk
4 thin sirloin steaks, total
  weight 750 g (1½ lb)
175 g (6 oz) mushrooms,
  sliced

50 g (2 oz) butter, cut into
  pieces
about 150 ml (¼ pint) hot
  chicken stock
50 g (2 oz) plain flour
salt
freshly ground black
  pepper
parsley sprig, to garnish

1. Place the celery, onion, carrot and milk in a large
jug. Cook, uncovered, for 3 minutes. Set aside to
infuse for 15 minutes. Strain and discard vegetables.
2. Place the steaks in a casserole dish and cook
uncovered for 6 minutes, turning over and
rearranging halfway through cooking. Set aside,
covered, while making the sauce.
3. Place the mushrooms in a medium bowl, cover
and cook for 3 minutes. Stir in the butter until
melted. Make up the meat juices to 150 ml (¼ pint)
with the stock, then stir in with the flour, strained
milk, and salt and pepper to taste. Cook, uncovered
for 5 minutes, stirring every minute.
4 Pour the sauce over the steaks. Cook, uncovered,
for 3 minutes. Garnish with the parsley.

MEATBALLS IN MUSHROOM & TOMATO SAUCE

Preparation time: about 15 minutes Cooking time: about 20 minutes
Microwave setting: Maximum (Full)

450 g (1 lb) minced beef
25 g (1 oz) fresh brown
   breadcrumbs
1 onion, peeled and grated
1 teaspoon dried mixed
   herbs
1 tablespoon tomato purée
salt
freshly ground black
   pepper
1 egg

Sauce:
40 g (1½ oz) butter
100 g (4 oz) mushrooms,
   finely chopped
350 g (12 oz) tomatoes,
   skinned and chopped
1 tablespoon tomato purée
40 g (1½ oz) plain flour
450 ml (¾ pint) hot beef
   stock
salt
freshly ground black
   pepper

1. Mix the beef, breadcrumbs, onion, herbs, tomato purée, salt and pepper together. Add the egg and mix well. Form the mixture into 16 balls.
2. Place the meatballs on a plate and cook for 2 minutes. Turn the meatballs over and turn the plate round. Cook for a further 2 minutes.
3. To make the sauce, place the butter, mushrooms, tomatoes and tomato purée in a medium bowl. Cover and cook for 5 minutes. Stir in the flour, then gradually add the hot stock. Cook for 2 minutes. Cool slightly.
4. Pour into a liquidizer and blend until smooth. Stir in the salt and pepper.
5. Place the meatballs in a bowl and pour over the sauce. Cook for 5 minutes. Serve with noodles and Parmesan cheese.

BEEFBURGER & ONION ROLLS

Preparation time: about 10 minutes Cooking time: about 12¾ minutes
Microwave setting: Maximum (Full)

1 medium onion, peeled
   and sliced
1 medium onion, peeled
   and grated
225 g (8 oz) minced beef
1 garlic clove, peeled and
   crushed
1 teaspoon dried mixed
   herbs

salt
freshly ground black
   pepper
25 g (1 oz) plain flour
4 soft rolls, cut in half
lettuce and tomatoes, to
   garnish

1. Place the sliced onion in a medium bowl. Cover and cook for 4 minutes. Set aside.
2. Place the grated onion in another medium bowl. Cover and cook for 3 minutes.
3. Stir in the minced beef, garlic, herbs, salt, pepper and flour. Divide into 4 and shape into patties.
4. Place on a plate and cook for 3 minutes. Turn the beefburgers over and turn the plate round. Cook for a further 2 minutes.
5. Place a few cooked onion slices on 4 of the roll halves. Place a beefburger on top and top with the remaining half roll.
6. Place on a plate and cook for 45 seconds. Garnish with lettuce and tomatoes.

SAVOURY MINCE WITH MIXED VEGETABLES

Preparation time: about 20 minutes Cooking time: about 17 minutes
Microwave setting: Maximum (Full)

1 large potato, peeled and diced
1 turnip, peeled and diced
1 carrot, peeled and sliced
1 medium onion, peeled and sliced
1 celery stick, chopped
450 g (1 lb) minced beef
1 teaspoon dried mixed herbs
1 tablespoon tomato purée
150 ml (¼ pint) hot beef stock
salt
freshly ground black pepper

1. Place the potato, turnip, carrot, onion and celery in a large bowl. Cover and cook for 10 minutes.
2. Stir in the beef, herbs, tomato purée, stock, and salt and pepper to taste. Cover and cook for 7 minutes, stirring halfway through cooking.
3. Serve with creamed potatoes.

Left: Meatballs in mushroom and tomato sauce; Beefburger and onion rolls.
Above: Savoury mince with mixed vegetables; Tomato cottage pie

TOMATO COTTAGE PIE

Preparation time: about 13 minutes Cooking time: about 24 minutes
Microwave setting: Maximum (Full)

750 g (1½ lb) potatoes, peeled and cut into 1 cm (½ inch) cubes
3 tablespoons water
1 medium onion, peeled and chopped
4 tablespoons tomato purée
2 tomatoes, skinned and chopped
450 g (1 lb) cooked beef, finely chopped
1 teaspoon dried mixed herbs
40 g (1½ oz) butter
½ teaspoon celery salt
150 ml (¼ pint) hot beef stock
freshly ground black pepper
2–3 tablespoons milk
salt
parsley sprigs, to garnish (optional)

1. Place the potatoes in a large bowl with the water. Cover and cook for 12 minutes, stirring halfway through cooking. Leave to stand, covered, while cooking the meat filling.
2. Place the onion in a round 1.2 litre (2 pint) casserole dish, cover and cook for 3½ minutes. Stir in the tomato purée, the chopped tomatoes, the beef, herbs, 25 g (1 oz) of the butter, the celery salt, stock and pepper to taste. Cover and cook for 4 minutes. Stir.
3. Meanwhile, mash the potatoes with the milk, remaining butter and season with salt and pepper to taste. Using a piping bag filled with a large star nozzle, pipe rosettes of the potato mixture over the meat. Cook, uncovered, for 4 minutes.
4. Garnish with parsley and serve with swedes.

SHEPHERD'S PIE

Preparation time: 15 minutes Cooking time: 26 minutes, plus grilling
Microwave setting: Maximum (Full)

1 kg (2 lb) potatoes, peeled and roughly diced into 2.5 cm (1 inch) cubes
3 tablespoons water
1 medium onion, peeled and thinly sliced
600 g (1¼ lb) minced beef
2 tablespoons tomato purée
½ teaspoon beef extract
¼ teaspoon chopped fresh parsley
¼ teaspoon dried oregano
¼ teaspoon dried marjoram
¼ teaspoon chopped fresh sage
1 teaspoon Worcestershire sauce
salt
freshly ground black pepper
4 tablespoons milk
25 g (1 oz) butter
parsley sprig, to garnish
gravy (page 53), to serve

1. Place the potatoes and water in a large bowl, cover and cook for 12 minutes. Stir once during cooking. Set aside, covered, while cooking the beef.
2. Place the onion in a large soufflé dish. Cover and cook for 4 minutes or until the onion is translucent.
3. Stir in the beef, tomato purée, beef extract, parsley, oregano, marjoram, sage, Worcestershire sauce and salt and pepper to taste. Cover and cook for 6 minutes. Stir to break up the mince with a fork halfway through cooking. Drain off the excess liquid.
4. Mash the potatoes with the milk, butter and salt and pepper to taste. Spread over the beef mixture and cook for 4 minutes. **Brown under a preheated conventional grill, if preferred.**
5. Garnish with parsley and serve with gravy.

MEAT LOAF

Preparation time: about 10 minutes, plus chilling
Cooking time: 12–14 minutes Microwave setting: Maximum (Full)

15 g (½ oz) butter
1 medium onion, peeled and finely chopped
225 g (8 oz) minced pork
225 g (8 oz) minced beef
1 garlic clove, peeled and crushed
7 tablespoons fresh white breadcrumbs
1 tablespoon tomato purée
¼ teaspoon celery salt
1 teaspoon dried mixed herbs
¼ teaspoon dried thyme
salt
freshly ground black pepper
1 egg, beaten

1. Place the butter and onion in a 900 ml (1½ pint) soufflé dish. Cover and cook for 4 minutes.
2. Mix together the pork, beef, garlic, breadcrumbs, tomato purée, celery salt, herbs, thyme, salt and pepper to taste. Stir in the onion and beaten egg.
3. Place in the soufflé dish. Cook, uncovered, for 4 minutes. Break up and stir with a fork. Cook, uncovered, for a further 4–6 minutes. Allow to cool.
4. Chill until cold. Turn out, slice and serve with a mixed green salad and sliced tomatoes.

Meat loaf; Shepherd's pie

ROAST LUNCH

Rollmops

Roast Beef
Boiled Potatoes
Green Beans
Gravy

Trifle

Order of cooking
1. Make the Rollmops (page 23) and Trifle (page 124) in advance.
2. Cook the beef.
3. While it is standing in foil, cook the potatoes (page 105) and leave to stand while cooking the green beans (page 105).
4. Leave the beans to stand while making the gravy.

Gravy: Roast beef: Boiled
potatoes; Green beans; Trifle;
Rollmops

ROAST BEEF

Preparation time: about 3 minutes
Cooking time: about 21 minutes, plus standing
Microwave setting: Maximum (Full)

1 × 1.5 kg (3 lb) joint of topside beef

1. Place the beef in a roasting bag. Pierce the bag and tie with a non-metallic tie.
2. Place the meat on a trivet or upturned saucer in a shallow dish. Cook for 21 minutes, turning over halfway through cooking.
3. Remove the bag, wrap the meat tightly in foil, shiny side inwards, and stand for 20 minutes.
4. Serve with boiled potatoes, green beans, gravy and horseradish sauce.

GRAVY

Preparation time: about 3 minutes Cooking time: about 2 minutes
Microwave setting: Maximum (Full)

2 tablespoons cold water
2 tablespoons meat
  sediment (from roasting
  bag)
1 tablespoon plain flour
300 ml ($\frac{1}{2}$ pint) hot beef
  stock
$\frac{1}{4}$ teaspoon gravy browning

1. Place the water in a jug. Stir in the meat sediment and flour. Add the stock and gravy browning.
2. Cook, uncovered, for 2 minutes, stirring twice.

Roast leg of lamb

LAMB

ROAST LEG OF LAMB

Preparation time: about 5 minutes
Cooking time: about 21 minutes, plus standing and grilling
Microwave setting: Maximum (Full)

1 × 1.5 kg (3 lb) leg of lamb, lightly beaten

1. Wrap a small piece of foil around the thin end of the lamb. Place the lamb in a roasting bag. Pierce the bag and tie with a non-metallic tie.
2. Place the lamb on a trivet or upturned saucer in a shallow dish. Cook for 21 minutes, turning over halfway through cooking.
3. Remove the lamb from the bag and wrap tightly in foil, shiny side inwards. Leave to stand for 20 minutes before carving. **Brown under a preheated conventional grill, if preferred.**
4. Serve with mint sauce, potatoes and vegetables.

NOISETTES OF LAMB

Preparation time: about 15 minutes Cooking time: about 17–18 minutes
Microwave setting: Maximum (Full)

8 lamb noisettes	25 g (1 oz) butter, diced
1 small carrot, peeled and thinly sliced	25 g (1 oz) plain flour
1 medium onion, peeled and chopped	about 300 ml ($\frac{1}{2}$ pint) hot chicken stock
1 celery stick, chopped	2 tablespoons tomato purée
25 g (1 oz) button mushrooms, sliced	150 ml ($\frac{1}{4}$ pint) red wine
1 teaspoon dried mixed herbs	salt
1 teaspoon dried rosemary	freshly ground black pepper
	parsley sprigs, to garnish

1. Place the noisettes in a shallow 1.5 litre (2$\frac{1}{2}$ pint) casserole dish. Cover with a piece of paper towel and cook for 7–8 minutes, turning over and rearranging halfway through cooking. Set aside, covered.
2. Place the carrot, onion, celery, mushrooms and herbs in a medium bowl. Cover and cook for 7 minutes, stirring halfway through cooking.
3. Stir in the butter until melted, then stir in the flour. Make up the meat juices to 300 ml ($\frac{1}{2}$ pint) with the stock, then stir in with the tomato purée, wine, and salt and pepper to taste. Cook, uncovered, for 4 minutes, stirring every minute.
4. Pour over the meat and cook for 3 minutes.
5. Garnish with the parsley and serve with boiled potatoes and broccoli.

LAMBS' KIDNEY CASSEROLE

Preparation time: about 25 minutes
Cooking time: about 14$\frac{1}{2}$ minutes, plus standing
Microwave setting: Maximum (Full)

1 medium onion, peeled and finely sliced	1 garlic clove, peeled and crushed
1 carrot, peeled and finely sliced	25 g (1 oz) cornflour
25 g (1 oz) butter	150 ml ($\frac{1}{4}$ pint) dry sherry
8 lambs' kidneys, halved, cores removed	300 ml ($\frac{1}{2}$ pint) hot beef stock
50 g (2 oz) mushrooms, sliced	1 tablespoon tomato purée
50 g (2 oz) frozen peas	4 small frankfurter sausages, sliced
2 tablespoons chopped fresh parsley	salt
	freshly ground black pepper

1. Place the onion, carrot and butter in a large bowl. Cover and cook for 4 minutes.
2. Stir in the kidneys, mushrooms, peas, half the parsley and the garlic. Cover and cook for 5$\frac{1}{2}$ minutes, stirring halfway through cooking.
3. Stir in the cornflour, sherry, hot stock, tomato purée, sausages, salt and pepper. Cover and cook for 5 minutes, stirring halfway through cooking.
4. Leave to stand, covered, for 3 minutes before serving, sprinkled with the remaining parsley.

From left to right: Noisettes of lamb; Lambs' kidney casserole; Liver and bacon casserole; Lamb chop casserole

LIVER & BACON CASSEROLE

Preparation time: about 20 minutes
Cooking time: about 16½ minutes, plus standing
Microwave setting: Maximum (Full)

4 streaky bacon rashers, rinds removed, chopped
25 g (1 oz) butter
1 carrot, peeled and thinly sliced
½ celery stick, finely chopped
1 medium onion, peeled and finely chopped
25 g (1 oz) cornflour
300 ml (½ pint) hot beef stock
225 g (8 oz) tomatoes, skinned and chopped

3 tablespoons tomato purée
1 teaspoon Worcestershire sauce
50 g (2 oz) mushrooms, chopped
1 teaspoon dried mixed herbs
2 bay leaves
salt
freshly ground black pepper
450 g (1 lb) lambs' liver, thinly sliced
bay leaves, to garnish

1. Place the bacon, butter, carrot, celery and onion in a large bowl. Cover and cook for 6½ minutes, stirring halfway through cooking.
2. Stir in the cornflour, then blend in the hot stock.
3. Add the tomatoes, tomato purée, Worcestershire sauce, mushrooms, herbs, bay leaves, salt, pepper and liver. Cover. Cook for 10 minutes, stirring halfway.
4. Leave to stand, covered, for 5 minutes. Garnish with bay leaves.

LAMB CHOP CASSEROLE

Preparation time: about 18 minutes Cooking time: about 28–31 minutes
Microwave setting: Maximum (Full)

8 lamb loin chops, total weight 1 kg (2 lb)
225 g (8 oz) potatoes, peeled and diced
1 large onion, peeled and chopped
2 large carrots, peeled and thinly sliced
1 small turnip, peeled and diced
2 courgettes, sliced

3 tablespoons cold water
25 g (1 oz) butter, cut into pieces
25 g (1 oz) plain flour
about 450 ml (¾ pint) hot chicken stock
½ teaspoon dried thyme
¼ teaspoon gravy browning
salt
freshly ground black pepper

1. Place the chops over the bottom and sides of a large bowl. Cover and cook for 6½–9½ minutes, rearranging halfway through cooking. Set aside, covered.
2. Place the potatoes, onion, carrot, turnip, courgettes and water in another large bowl. Cover and cook for 13 minutes or until tender, stirring halfway through.
3. Stir in the butter until melted. Stir in the flour. Make up the meat juices to 450 ml (¾ pint) with the stock, then stir in with the thyme, gravy browning, and salt and pepper. Cover and cook for 4 minutes, stirring halfway through cooking.
4. Fold in the chops. Cook, uncovered, for 4 minutes.

LAMB CHOPS WITH SPICY SAUCE

Preparation time: about 10 minutes Cooking time: about 11½ minutes
Microwave setting: Maximum (Full)

l small onion, peeled and
  finely sliced
50 g (2 oz) butter
4 chump lamb chops
l tablespoon molasses
  sugar
l teaspoon Worcestershire
  sauce

l teaspoon soy sauce
l garlic clove, peeled and
  crushed
4 tablespoons tomato
  purée
salt
freshly ground black
  pepper

1. Place the onion and butter in a small bowl. Cover and cook for 3½ minutes.
2. Place the chops in a shallow casserole. Cover with a piece of paper towel and cook for 5 minutes. Check if cooked to taste. Cook for 1 more minute if necessary.
3. Pour off the fat collected in the casserole.
4. While the chops are cooking, mix the onion and butter with the sugar, Worcestershire sauce, soy sauce, garlic, tomato purée, salt and pepper.
5. Spoon the sauce over the chops in the casserole, cover and cook for a further 3 minutes.
6. Serve with boiled rice and sweetcorn.

LAMB WITH CHERRIES

Preparation time: about 10 minutes Cooking time: about 17½ minutes
Microwave setting: Maximum (Full)

4 lamb fillets, total weight
  750 g (1½ lb), lightly
  beaten
l medium onion, peeled
  and chopped
25 g (1 oz) butter, cut into
  pieces
450 g (1 lb) frozen black
  pitted cherries, thawed
  and drained (no sugar
  added)

l teaspoon dried marjoram
salt
about 300 ml (½ pint) hot
  chicken stock
25 g (1 oz) cornflour

1. Place the fillets over the bottom and sides of a large bowl. Cover and cook for 6½ minutes, rearranging halfway through cooking. Set aside, covered.
2. Place the onion in a medium bowl, cover and cook for 3 minutes. Stir in the butter until melted. Stir in the cherries, marjoram and a little salt, cover and cook for 3 minutes.
3. Make up the meat juices to 300 ml (½ pint) with the stock, then stir into the onion and cherries with the cornflour. Cook, uncovered, for 5 minutes, stirring occasionally.
4. Arrange the fillets in a shallow serving dish and pour over the sauce. Cook, uncovered, for 3 minutes. Serve with piped creamed potatoes.

Clockwise: Lamb with Mozzarella
cheese; Sweet and sour lamb;
Lamb with cherries; Lamb chops
with spicy sauce

LAMB WITH MOZZARELLA CHEESE

Preparation time: about 5 minutes, plus marinating overnight
Cooking time: about 6–7 minutes Microwave setting: Maximum (Full)

8 lamb cutlets
100 g (4 oz) Mozzarella
  cheese, thinly sliced

Marinade:
2 tablespoons white wine
  vinegar
150 ml (¼ pint) dry sherry
2 teaspoons dark brown
  sugar

l tablespoon orange juice
¼ teaspoon Worcestershire
  sauce
salt
freshly ground black
  pepper
l tablespoon chopped
  parsley, to garnish

1. Mix together the vinegar, sherry, sugar, orange juice, Worcestershire sauce, and salt and pepper.
2. Arrange the cutlets in a shallow dish. Pour over the marinade and add sufficient cold water to cover the cutlets. Leave to marinate for about 24 hours.
3. Drain the marinade off the cutlets. Cover the cutlets with a piece of paper towel. Cook for 4–5 minutes, rearranging halfway through cooking.
4. Pour off the juice and overlap the cutlets to look attractive. Cover the cutlets with the cheese. Cook, uncovered, for 2 minutes.
5. Sprinkle with chopped parsley to garnish.

SWEET & SOUR LAMB

Preparation time: about 18 minutes Cooking time: about 18 minutes
Microwave setting: Maximum (Full)

4 lamb loin chops, total
  weight 600 g (1¼ lb)
l medium onion, peeled
  and chopped
½ green pepper, cored,
  seeded and finely
  chopped
½ red pepper, cored,
  seeded and finely
  chopped
½ teaspoon dried rosemary
½ teaspoon dried marjoram
½ teaspoon dried parsley

l garlic clove, peeled and
  crushed
25 g (1 oz) butter, cut into
  pieces
25 g (1 oz) plain flour
300 ml (½ pint) hot chicken
  stock
2 tablespoons white wine
  vinegar
l tablespoon soy sauce
50 g (2 oz) brown sugar
salt
freshly ground black
  pepper

1. Place the chops in a shallow 1.5 litre (2½ pint) casserole dish, cover with a piece of paper towel and cook for 7 minutes, turning over and rearranging halfway through cooking. Set aside, covered.
2. Place the onion, peppers, rosemary, marjoram, parsley and garlic in a medium bowl. Cover and cook for 5 minutes, stirring halfway through.
3. Stir in the butter until melted. Stir in the flour. Make up the meat juices to 300 ml (½ pint) with the stock, then blend into the vegetables with the vinegar, soy sauce, sugar, and salt and pepper to taste. Cook, uncovered, for 3 minutes, stirring every minute.
4. Pour the sauce over the chops and cook, uncovered, for 3 minutes.
5. Serve with buttered noodles.

CROWN ROAST OF LAMB

Preparation time: about 10 minutes Cooking time: about 29 minutes, plus standing Microwave Setting: Maximum (Full)

1 medium onion, peeled and finely chopped
50 g (2 oz) butter, cut into pieces
1 garlic clove, peeled and crushed
meat trimmings (from preparing crown roast), finely chopped
100 g (4 oz) fresh white breadcrumbs
¼ teaspoon dried marjoram
¼ teaspoon dried basil
¼ teaspoon dried parsley
¼ teaspoon celery salt
freshly ground black pepper
1 egg, lightly beaten
1 crown roast of lamb, prepared weight 1.1 kg (2¼ lb), comprising 12 chops
12 glacé cherries, to garnish

To prepare crown roast:
Bend each rack into a semi-circle, fat inwards, cutting between, but not dividing chops, if necessary. Sew ends together to form a circle.
1. Place the onion, butter, garlic and meat trimmings in a medium bowl. Cover and cook for 4 minutes.
2. Stir in the breadcrumbs, marjoram, basil, parsley, celery salt, and pepper to taste. Bind with the egg.
3. Stuff the centre of the roast and stand on a trivet or upturned saucer. Cook, uncovered, for 25 minutes, turning round halfway through cooking.
4. Wrap tightly in foil and stand for 20–25 minutes.
5. Place a cherry on top of each bone to garnish.

LAMB IN CREAM & CIDER

Preparation time: about 20 minutes Cooking time: about 17½ minutes Microwave setting: Maximum (Full)

8 lamb loin chops, total weight 1 kg (2 lb)
1 medium onion, peeled and chopped
½ green pepper, cored, seeded and chopped
225 g (8 oz) mushrooms, sliced
1 teaspoon dried rosemary
25 g (1 oz) butter, cut into pieces
about 65 ml (2½ fl oz) hot chicken stock
25 g (1 oz) plain flour
225 ml (7½ fl oz) dry cider
salt
freshly ground black pepper
4 tablespoons double cream
chopped parsley, to garnish

1. Place the chops around the bottom and sides of a large bowl, cover and cook for 6½ minutes, rearranging halfway through. Set aside, covered.
2. Place the onion and green pepper in a large bowl, cover and cook for 4 minutes. Stir in the mushrooms, rosemary and butter. Cover and cook for 3 minutes.
3. Make up the meat juices to 65 ml (2½ fl oz) with the stock, then stir in with the flour, cider, and salt and pepper. Add the chops. Cover and cook for 4 minutes, stirring halfway through.
4. Skim if necessary, then stir in the cream and reheat for 1 minute if necessary. Sprinkle with chopped parsley, to garnish. Serve with green beans and savoury rice.

Crown roast of lamb; Lamb in cream and cider

LAMB CURRY

Preparation time: about 15 minutes Cooking time: about 14 minutes
Microwave Setting: Maximum (Full)

1 medium onion, peeled
  and chopped
1 garlic clove, peeled and
  crushed
1 tablespoon ground
  coriander
1 teaspoon turmeric
$\frac{1}{2}$ teaspoon ground cumin
$\frac{1}{4}$ teaspoon chilli powder
$\frac{1}{4}$ teaspoon ground
  cinnamon
$\frac{1}{4}$ teaspoon ground ginger
$\frac{1}{4}$ teaspoon grated nutmeg
1 tablespoon plain flour
1 tablespoon tomato purée

1 teaspoon lemon juice
1 tablespoon desiccated
  coconut
$\frac{1}{4}$ teaspoon meat extract
25 g (1 oz) sultanas
450 ml ($\frac{3}{4}$ pint) hot chicken
  stock
2 teaspoons curry paste
750 g ($1\frac{1}{2}$ lb) boneless
  cooked lamb, finely
  chopped
salt
freshly ground black
  pepper

1. Place the onion, garlic, coriander, turmeric, cumin, chilli powder, cinnamon, ginger and nutmeg in a large bowl. Cover and cook for 4 minutes.
2. Stir in the flour, tomato purée, lemon juice, coconut, meat extract, sultanas, stock, curry paste and lamb. Season to taste with salt and pepper. Cover and cook for 10 minutes, stirring twice.
3. Serve with rice, sliced tomatoes, sliced bananas, mango chutney and desiccated coconut.

MOUSSAKA

Preparation time: about 20 minutes, plus standing
Cooking time: about 29 minutes Microwave setting: Maximum (Full)

1 large aubergine, cut into
  5 mm ($\frac{1}{4}$ inch) slices
salt
25 g (1 oz) butter
2 medium onions, peeled
  and finely sliced
2 garlic cloves, peeled and
  crushed
450 g (1 lb) lamb, minced
3 tablespoons tomato
  purée
1 teaspoon dried mixed
  herbs

25 g (1 oz) plain flour
150 ml ($\frac{1}{4}$ pint) beef stock
freshly ground black
  pepper

Sauce:
25 g (1 oz) butter
25 g (1 oz) plain flour
300 ml ($\frac{1}{2}$ pint) milk
50 g (2 oz) Cheddar
  cheese, grated
1 teaspoon dry mustard
1 egg, beaten

1. Place the aubergine slices in a colander and sprinkle with salt. Leave for 30 minutes to remove excess liquid. Rinse under cold water and drain.
2. Place the aubergine slices in a medium bowl, cover and cook for 3 minutes. Set aside.
3. Place the butter, onions and garlic in a large bowl. Cover and cook for 3 minutes or until translucent.
4. Stir in the lamb, cover and cook for 4 minutes.
5. Stir in the tomato purée, herbs, flour, stock, salt and pepper. Cover Cook for 12 minutes. Set aside.
6. To make the sauce, place the butter in a 600 ml (1 pint) jug. Cook for $\frac{3}{4}$ minute or until melted. Blend in the flour and milk. Cook for $2\frac{1}{2}$ minutes, stirring twice. Stir in the cheese, mustard and beaten egg.
7. Make alternate layers of lamb and aubergine slices in a large shallow oblong casserole. Pour over the sauce and cook for 5 minutes.

STUFFED LEG OF LAMB

Preparation time: about 15 minutes
Cooking time: about 18 minutes, plus standing
Microwave setting: Maximum (Full)

1 small onion, peeled and
  finely chopped
25 g (1 oz) butter
75 g (3 oz) fresh white
  breadcrumbs
1 tablespoon dried mint or
  2 tablespoons chopped
  fresh mint

salt
freshly ground black
  pepper
1 egg, beaten
1 kg (2 lb) boned leg of
  lamb

1. Place the onion and butter in a large bowl. Cover and cook for 2 minutes.
2. Stir in the breadcrumbs, mint, salt and pepper. Add the egg and mix well.
3. Lay the boned leg of lamb out flat. Spread the stuffing over the meat, roll up and secure.
4. Wrap in cling film and place on an upturned saucer in a large dish. Cook for 16 minutes.
5. Remove cling film and wrap the meat in foil, then leave for 15 minutes before carving.

STUFFED BREAST OF LAMB

Preparation time: about 20 minutes
Cooking time: about 11 minutes, plus standing and grilling
Microwave setting: Maximum (Full)

1 medium onion, peeled
  and chopped
25 g (1 oz) butter
100 g (4 oz) fresh white
  breadcrumbs
1 teaspoon dried mixed
  herbs

1 teaspoon dried rosemary
grated rind of 1 orange
1 tablespoon orange juice
salt
freshly ground pepper
1 × 450 g (1 lb) boned
  breast of lamb

1. Place the onion and butter in a medium bowl, cover and cook for 3 minutes. Stir in the breadcrumbs, herbs, orange rind and juice, and salt and pepper to taste.
2. Spread the stuffing over the breast, roll up and secure with string. Stand in a shallow dish and cook, uncovered, for 8 minutes, turning over halfway through cooking.
3. Wrap in foil and stand for 10 minutes before serving, with new potatoes and peas. For a crispy finish, **brown under a preheated conventional grill.**

DINNER PARTY

Liver Pâté

Guard of Honour
Vichy Carrots
Sweetcorn

Cold Strawberry Soufflé

Order of cooking

1. Make the pâté (page 28) and soufflé (page 120), and prepare the guard in advance.
2. Cook the Guard of Honour and while it is standing in foil, cook the carrots (page 105).
3. Leave to stand while cooking the sweetcorn (page 105).

Left: Stuffed leg of lamb; Stuffed breast of lamb. Above: Guard of honour; Sweetcorn; Vichy carrots; Cold strawberry soufflé; Liver pâté

GUARD OF HONOUR

Preparation time: about 20 minutes
Cooking time: about 25 minutes, plus standing
Microwave setting: Maximum (Full)

25 g (1 oz) butter
1 small onion, peeled and chopped
¼ teaspoon chopped fresh marjoram
¼ teaspoon chopped fresh rosemary
¼ teaspoon chopped fresh sage
1 tablespoon chopped fresh parsley

75 g (3 oz) fresh white breadcrumbs
salt
freshly ground black pepper
1 egg, beaten
1 guard of honour, prepared weight 750 g (1½ lb), each rack comprising 6 chops

To prepare guard:

With fat on the outside, ease and push racks together to interlock the rib bones. Sew or tie bases.
1. Place the butter, onion, marjoram, rosemary, sage and parsley in a small bowl. Cover and cook for 3 minutes. Stir in the breadcrumbs, and salt and pepper to taste. Bind with the egg.
2. Stuff the guard and place in a shallow dish. Cook for 22 minutes, turning round halfway through.
3. Wrap tightly in foil and stand for 15–20 minutes.

Roast pork

PORK, BACON & HAM

ROAST PORK

Preparation time: about 4 minutes
Cooking time: about 30 minutes, plus standing and grilling
Microwave setting: Maximum (Full)

1 tablespoon oil	$\frac{1}{2}$ teaspoon salt
1 × 1.5 kg (3 lb) fillet half leg of pork, scored	

If an exact 1.5 kg (3 lb) fillet is not available, check the chart on page 12 for cooking times per 450 g (1 lb).

1. Rub the oil into the fat on the meat, then rub in the salt. Place the meat in a shallow dish with the fat uppermost. Cover with a paper towel. Cook for 30 minutes. Remove the towel after 15 minutes.

2. Wrap the meat in foil, shiny side inwards, and leave for 15–20 minutes before carving. If desired, **brown under a preheated conventional grill**.

3. Serve with potatoes, peas, carrots, stuffing, apple sauce and gravy.

PORK CASSEROLE

Preparation time: about 10 minutes Cooking time: about 16–18 minutes
Microwave setting: Maximum (Full)

450 g (1 lb) pork fillet,
 diced to 2.5 cm (1 inch)
 pieces
1 onion, peeled and finely
 chopped
2 carrots, peeled and thinly
 sliced
1 red pepper, cored,
 seeded and chopped
1 garlic clove, peeled and
 crushed
$\frac{1}{4}$ teaspoon ground mace
$\frac{1}{4}$ teaspoon dried thyme
$\frac{1}{4}$ teaspoon dried sage

$\frac{1}{4}$ teaspoon dried parsley
2 tablespoons tomato
 purée
25 g (1 oz) butter, cut into
 pieces
25 g (1 oz) plain flour
about 300 ml ($\frac{1}{2}$ pint)
 chicken stock
1 × 200 g (7 oz) can
 sweetcorn kernels,
 drained
salt
freshly ground black
 pepper

1. Place the pork in a shallow dish, cover and cook for 4–6 minutes, stirring halfway through cooking. Set aside, covered.
2. Place the onion, carrot, red pepper, garlic, mace, thyme, sage, parsley and tomato purée in a medium bowl. Cover and cook for 8 minutes, stirring halfway through cooking.

3. Stir in the butter until melted. Stir in the flour. Make up the meat juices to 300 ml ($\frac{1}{2}$ pint) with stock, then stir in with the sweetcorn, pork and salt and pepper. Cook, uncovered, for 4 minutes, stirring every minute.
4. Serve with creamed potatoes and mange-touts.

From left to right: Pork casserole; Pork chops with apple; Pork chops with oregano and tomato sauce

PORK CHOPS WITH APPLE

Preparation time: about 10 minutes
Cooking time: about 9 minutes, plus standing
Microwave setting: Maximum (Full)

2 teaspoons soy sauce	freshly ground black
2 teaspoons	pepper
Worcestershire sauce	4 pork chops
50 g (2 oz) butter	1 large eating apple,
25 g (1 oz) soft dark brown	peeled, cored and cut
sugar	into 4 slices
salt	

1. Place the soy sauce, Worcestershire sauce, butter, sugar, salt and pepper in a 300 ml (½ pint) jug. Cook for 1 minute. Stir the sauce.
2. Brush both sides of the chops and apple slices with the sauce.
3. Arrange the pork chops in a shallow casserole. Cover and cook for 4 minutes. Turn the chops over and turn the casserole round.
4. Brush the chops with any remaining sauce and place a slice of apple on each one. Cover and cook for 4 minutes.
5. Leave to stand, covered, for 3 minutes.

PORK CHOPS WITH OREGANO & TOMATO SAUCE

Preparation time: about 7 minutes Cooking time: about 17–19 minutes
Microwave setting: Maximum (Full)

4 pork loin chops, total	1 × 400 g (14 oz) can
weight 750 g (1½ lb)	tomatoes
1 medium onion, peeled	1 tablespoon tomato purée
and finely chopped	1 tablespoon chopped
1 teaspoon dried oregano	fresh parsley
25 g (1 oz) butter, cut into	200 ml (7 fl oz) hot chicken
pieces	stock
25 g (1 oz) cornflour	salt
	freshly ground pepper

1. Place the chops around a medium bowl, cover and cook for 7 minutes, rearranging halfway through cooking. Set aside, covered.
2. Place the onion and oregano in a large bowl, cover and cook for 4 minutes, stirring halfway through.
3. Stir in the butter until melted. Stir in the cornflour, undrained tomatoes, tomato purée, parsley, stock, and salt and pepper to taste. Cover and cook for 3–5 minutes, stirring halfway through cooking.
4. Add drained chops. Cook, uncovered, for 3 minutes.

GARLIC BACON STICKS

Preparation time: about 10 minutes Cooking time: about 5½ minutes Microwave setting: Maximum (Full)

1 garlic clove
8 streaky bacon rashers,
  rinds removed and
  stretched

8 grissini (bread sticks)
25 g (1 oz) Cheddar
  cheese, finely grated

1. Rub the garlic over each rasher of bacon.
2. Twist a rasher of bacon around the top half of each bread stick. Place the sticks on a piece of paper towel on a plate. Cook, uncovered, for 5½ minutes or until the bacon is cooked.
3. Twirl the hot bacon in the cheese to coat on all sides.
4. Serve hot or cold with drinks.

Glazed bacon joint; Garlic bacon
sticks

GLAZED BACON JOINT

Preparation time: about 5 minutes Cooking time: about 27½ minutes, plus standing and grilling Microwave setting: Maximum (Full)

1.5 kg (3 lb) unsmoked fore
  end bacon joint, soaked
  overnight and drained

2 tablespoons marmalade

1. Place the bacon joint in a roasting bag and secure with a non-metallic tie. Prick the bag and place the bacon in a shallow dish. Cook for 13½ minutes. Turn the bacon over and cook for a further 13½ minutes.
2. Remove the bacon joint from the bag and wrap tightly in foil. Leave to stand for 15 minutes.
3. Place the marmalade in a small bowl and heat for 30 seconds.
4. Place the bacon in a grill pan and spread the marmalade over the top of the joint. **Cook under a preheated conventional grill** until bubbling.

PORK WITH ORANGE & CRANBERRIES

Preparation time: about 10 minutes Cooking time: about 17-20 minutes
Microwave setting: Maximum (Full) and Defrost

4 pork fillets, total weight 750 g (1½ lb)	25 g (1 oz) caster sugar
grated rind of 1 orange	225 g (8 oz) fresh cranberries
125 ml (4 fl oz) orange juice	4 orange slices, to garnish

1. Place the fillets in a shallow dish, cover and cook on Maximum for 6-9 minutes, rearranging them halfway through cooking. Set aside, covered.
2. Place the orange rind and juice, sugar and cranberries in a medium bowl. Cover and cook on Maximum for 2½ minutes. Stir, re-cover and cook for 5½ minutes on Defrost.
3. Drain the fillets and spoon the cranberry mixture over them. Cook, uncovered, for 3 minutes on Maximum.
4. Cut into slices and garnish with orange.

Pork with orange and cranberries; Pork fillets in wine sauce

PORK FILLETS IN WINE SAUCE

Preparation time: about 10 minutes Cooking time: about 16½–19½ minutes
Microwave setting: Maximum (Full)

4 pork fillets, total weight 750 g (1½ lb)	25 g (1 oz) plain flour
1 medium onion, peeled and chopped	about 150 ml (¼ pint) hot chicken stock
100 g (4 oz) button mushrooms, sliced	150 ml (¼ pint) rosé wine
1 celery stick, sliced	salt
¼ teaspoon dried parsley	freshly ground black pepper
¼ teaspoon dried sage	
¼ teaspoon dried tarragon	**To garnish:**
25 g (1 oz) butter, diced	fried apple rings
	parsley sprigs

1. Place the pork fillets in a shallow dish, cover and cook for 6–9 minutes, turning over and rearranging halfway through cooking. Set aside, covered.
2. Place the onion, mushrooms, celery, parsley, sage and tarragon in a medium bowl. Cover and cook for 5½ minutes.
3. Stir in the butter until melted. Stir in the flour. Make up the meat juices to 150 ml (¼ pint) with stock, then stir in with the wine and salt and pepper. Cook, covered, for 2 minutes, stirring after 1 minute.
4. Add the fillets and turn to coat with the sauce. Cook, covered, for 3 minutes.
5. Garnish with the apple rings and parsley sprigs. Serve with new potatoes and fried courgettes.

GAMMON IN CIDER

Preparation time: about 10 minutes Cooking time: about 15 minutes
Microwave setting: Maximum (Full)

600 g (1¼ lb) gammon,
  cubed
1 medium onion, peeled
  and chopped
1 celery stick, chopped
1 teaspoon dried marjoram
2 red eating apples, cored
  and sliced

25 g (1 oz) butter, cut into
  pieces
25 g (1 oz) cornflour
150 ml (¼ pint) hot chicken
  stock
300 ml (½ pint) dry cider
freshly ground black
  pepper

1. Place the gammon in a shallow dish, cover and
cook for 4 minutes, stirring halfway through
cooking. Remove the gammon with its juices and set
aside, covered.
2. Add the onion, celery and marjoram to the dish,
cover and cook for 3 minutes.
3. Stir in the apples, cover and cook for 2 minutes.
4. Stir in the butter until melted. Stir in the cornflour,
stock, cider and pepper to taste. Cook, uncovered,
for 3 minutes, until thickened, stirring every minute.
5. Replace the gammon and its juices and heat
through for about 3 minutes.
6. Serve with boiled potatoes and broccoli.

BACON & VEGETABLE CASSEROLE

Preparation time: about 15 minutes Cooking time: about 20 minutes
Microwave setting: Maximum (Full)

½ green pepper, cored,
  seeded and thinly sliced
225 g (8 oz) onion, peeled
  and thinly sliced into
  rings
275 g (10 oz) potato, peeled
  and diced
1 celery stick, chopped
100 g (4 oz) carrot, peeled
  and thinly sliced
100 g (4 oz) frozen
  cauliflower florets

12 streaky bacon rashers,
  derinded, stretched,
  rolled and secured with
  wooden cocktail sticks
25 g (1 oz) plain flour
450 ml (¾ pint) hot chicken
  stock
1 teaspoon dried mixed
  herbs
salt
freshly ground black
  pepper

1. Place the green pepper, onion, potato, celery,
carrot and cauliflower in a large bowl. Cover and
cook for 10 minutes, stirring twice during cooking.
2. Place the bacon rolls on the top of the vegetables,
cover and cook for 5 minutes.
3. Remove the bacon. Stir in the flour, stock, herbs,
and salt and pepper to taste. Cook, uncovered, for 3
minutes. Serve straightaway.

4. Remove the sticks from the bacon rolls. Stir the bacon into the vegetables. Cook, uncovered, for 2 minutes. Serve immediately as a complete supper dish.

Variation:
Use red or yellow peppers in place of the green pepper, and swedes or turnips in place of the carrots.

Homemade chicken stock will give the casserole a richer flavour.

From left to right: Gammon in cider; Bacon and vegetable casserole; Gammon steaks with pineapple

GAMMON STEAKS WITH PINEAPPLE

Preparation time: about 5 minutes
Cooking time: about 13 minutes, plus standing
Microwave setting: Maximum (Full)

4 gammon slices, total weight 1 kg (2 lb)

4 slices of canned pineapple, drained and cut in half

1. Arrange the gammon slices over the bottom and sides of a large bowl. Cover and cook for 10 minutes, rearranging halfway through cooking.
2. Pour off the juice and arrange the gammon in a serving dish. Arrange the pineapple halves over the gammon. Cook, uncovered, for 3 minutes.
3. Cover the dish with foil and stand for 4 minutes before serving. Serve with sauté potatoes.

PAPRIKA PORK CHOPS

Preparation time: about 10 minutes Cooking time: about 16–19 minutes
Microwave setting: Maximum (Full)

4 pork spare rib chops, total weight 750 g (1½ lb)	¼ teaspoon dried oregano
½ green pepper, cored, seeded and sliced	¼ teaspoon dried basil
½ red pepper, cored, seeded and sliced	25 g (1 oz) butter, cut into pieces
1 celery stick, chopped	25 g (1 oz) cornflour
¼ teaspoon Worcestershire sauce	about 450 ml (¾ pint) hot chicken stock
2 tablespoons tomato purée	salt
1 tablespoon paprika	freshly ground black pepper
	2 tablespoons soured cream

1. Place the chops in a shallow dish, cover and cook for 6–9 minutes, turning over and rearranging halfway through cooking. Set aside, covered.
2. Place the peppers, celery, Worcestershire sauce, tomato purée, paprika, oregano and basil in a medium bowl. Cover and cook for 5 minutes, stirring halfway through cooking.
3. Stir in the butter until melted. Stir in the cornflour. Make up the meat juices to 450 ml (¾ pint) with stock, then stir in with salt and pepper to taste. Cook, uncovered for 2 minutes, stirring after 1 minute.
4. Add the chops and cook, uncovered, for 3 minutes. Stir in the soured cream.
5. Serve with plain boiled rice and sweetcorn.

COLD CURRIED PORK

Preparation time: about 20 minutes, plus cooling and chilling
Cooking time: about 5–7 minutes Microwave setting: Maximum (Full)

450 g (1 lb) pork fillet, cubed	1 carrot, peeled and grated
2 eating apples, cored and diced	25 g (1 oz) sultanas
2 spring onions, trimmed and chopped	25 g (1 oz) roasted peanuts
½ red pepper, cored, seeded and chopped	1 celery stick, chopped
½ small cucumber, peeled and diced	1 tablespoon mild curry powder
	225 ml (8 fl oz) mayonnaise
	salt
	freshly ground black pepper
	spring onions, to garnish

1. Place the pork in a large bowl, cover and cook for 5–7 minutes, stirring halfway through cooking. Leave to stand, covered, until cold. Drain.
2. Mix together the apples, spring onions, red pepper, cucumber, carrot, sultanas, peanuts and celery.
3. Mix together the curry powder, mayonnaise, and salt and pepper to taste. Stir in the pork and the fruit and vegetable mixture. Chill. Garnish with spring onions.

Clockwise: Spare ribs with barbecue sauce; Pork kebabs; Cold curried pork; Paprika pork chops

SPARE RIBS WITH BARBECUE SAUCE

Preparation time: about 5 minutes Cooking time: about 28½ minutes
Microwave setting: Maximum (Full)

15 g (½ oz) butter	1 tablespoon clear honey
1 garlic clove, peeled and crushed	1 tablespoon soy sauce
1 medium onion, peeled and finely chopped	1 tablespoon dark brown sugar
1 × 400 g (14 oz) can tomatoes, drained	salt
1 tablespoon dried mixed herbs	freshly ground black pepper
2 tablespoons Worcestershire sauce	750 g (1½ lb) pork spare ribs

1. Place the butter, garlic and onion in a large shallow bowl. Cover and cook for 3½ minutes.
2. Stir in the tomatoes, herbs, Worcestershire sauce, honey, soy sauce, sugar, salt and pepper. Cover and cook for 5 minutes.
3. Add spare ribs. Cover and cook for 10 minutes.
4. Rearrange the spare ribs and baste with the sauce. Cook for a further 10 minutes or to taste.

PORK KEBABS

Preparation time: about 15 minutes, plus marinating
Cooking time: about 13 minutes Microwave setting: Maximum (Full)

Marinade:	Kebabs:
3 tablespoons olive oil	450 g (1 lb) pork fillet, cut into 4 cm (1½ inch) cubes
150 ml (¼ pint) water	½ red pepper, cored, seeded and cut into 8 pieces
2 tablespoons Worcestershire sauce	½ green pepper, cored, seeded and cut into 8 pieces
1 small onion, peeled and sliced	2 tomatoes, halved
1 tablespoon white wine vinegar	
1 teaspoon dried mixed herbs	**Sauce:**
1 tablespoon redcurrant jelly	25 g (1 oz) butter
salt	25 g (1 oz) plain flour
freshly ground black pepper	150 ml (¼ pint) hot chicken stock
	2 tablespoons tomato purée

1. Mix together the marinade ingredients, with salt and pepper to taste, in a shallow dish. Add the pork cubes and turn to coat. Leave for 2 hours.
2. Place the peppers in a medium bowl, cover and cook for 2 minutes.
3. Drain the pork cubes, reserving the marinade. Thread the pork cubes and pepper pieces alternately on to 4 wooden skewers. Place on a plate and cover with paper towels. Cook for 3 minutes.
4. Place half a tomato on each skewer, cover again and cook for 4 minutes. Set aside.
5. Place the butter in a large jug and cook, uncovered, for 1 minute or until melted. Stir in the flour. Blend in the strained, reserved marinade, hot chicken stock and tomato purée. Cook for 3 minutes, stirring every minute.

PICNIC HAM PÂTÉ

Preparation time: about 6 minutes, plus cooling
Cooking time: about 7½ minutes Microwave setting: Maximum (Full)

50 g (2 oz) mushrooms
100 g (4 oz) onions, peeled
  and quartered
350 g (12 oz) lean ham,
  roughly chopped
1 garlic clove, peeled
¼ teaspoon dried sage
¼ teaspoon dried parsley
¼ teaspoon dried rosemary

¼ teaspoon dried marjoram
freshly ground black
  pepper
2 eggs, lightly beaten

To garnish:
lettuce
tomato slices

1. Process or finely mince the mushrooms, onions,
ham, garlic, sage, parsley, rosemary, marjoram and
pepper to taste. Bind the mixture with the eggs.
2. Line a 16 cm (6½ inch) diameter soufflé dish with
cling film and place an inexpensive tumbler upside-
down in the centre. Spread the ham mixture evenly
over the bottom.
3. Cover and cook for 7½ minutes, turning round
halfway through cooking. Leave to cool before
turning out.
4. Garnish with lettuce and sliced tomatoes and
serve with potato salad.

FRANKFURTERS WRAPPED IN BACON

Preparation time: about 5 minutes Cooking time: about 4 minutes
Microwave setting: Maximum (Full)

8 streaky bacon rashers,
  rinds removed

8 large frankfurters
parsley sprigs, to garnish

1. Wind the bacon around the frankfurters. Place in a
circle on a plate. Cover with a paper towel and cook
for 4 minutes.
2. Garnish with parsley and serve with potato salad.

Left: Picnic ham pâté;
Frankfurters wrapped in bacon.
Right, clockwise: Jellied ham and
chicken; Baked bananas; Stuffed
loin of pork; Croquette potatoes;
Apple sauce; Broccoli with
cheese sauce

DINNER PARTY

Jellied Ham and Chicken

Stuffed Pork Loin
Croquette Potatoes
Broccoli with Cheese Sauce
Apple Sauce

Baked Bananas

Order of cooking
1. Earlier in the day, make the jellied ham and chicken (page 25), croquette potatoes (page 102) and apple sauce (page 139). Prepare the pork for cooking.
2. Cook the loin and while standing, cook the broccoli, the sauce (page 106), then the baked bananas (page 126).
3. Reheat the potatoes and apple sauce just before serving. They will take 3 minutes each, or 6 minutes if put in the cooker together (but check the apple sauce and remove it as soon as it is hot).

STUFFED PORK LOIN

Preparation time: about 20 minutes, plus standing and grilling
Cooking time: about 14–17 minutes Microwave setting: Maximum (Full)

1 small onion, peeled and finely chopped	$\frac{1}{4}$ teaspoon dried rosemary
1 garlic clove, peeled and crushed	$\frac{1}{4}$ teaspoon dried thyme
25 g (1 oz) butter	salt
25 g (1 oz) fresh white breadcrumbs	freshly ground black pepper
grated rind of 1 lemon	1 × 1 kg (2 lb) boned loin of pork, skin scored

1. Place the onion, garlic and butter in a bowl. Cover and cook for 3 minutes. Stir in the breadcrumbs, lemon rind, rosemary, thyme, and salt and pepper to taste.
2. Spread the stuffing over the loin, close up and secure with string. Place in a shallow dish, skin uppermost, and cook, uncovered, for 11–14 minutes, turning round halfway through cooking.
3. Wrap tightly in foil and stand for 10 minutes before carving. If desired, **brown the loin under a preheated conventional grill.**

Devilled chicken drumsticks;
Turkey breasts Cordon Bleu

POULTRY & GAME

DEVILLED CHICKEN DRUMSTICKS

Preparation time: about 5 minutes Cooking time: about 12½ minutes
Microwave setting: Maximum (Full)

8 chicken drumsticks, total
  weight 750 g (1½ lb)
1 teaspoon curry powder
1 tablespoon soy sauce
3 tablespoons tomato
  purée

3 tablespoons dark soft
  brown sugar
25 g (1 oz) butter, cut into
  pieces
spring onions, to garnish

1. Place the drumsticks in the bottom of a shallow
oblong casserole dish. Cook, uncovered, for 4½
minutes. Set aside.
2. Place the curry powder, soy sauce, tomato
purée, sugar and butter in a jug. Cook, uncovered
for 1½ minutes.
3. Rearrange the drumsticks and brush with the
sauce. Cook, uncovered, for 4½ minutes.
4. Brush the remaining sauce over the drumsticks
and cook for 2 minutes. Garnish with spring onions.
5. Serve with rice and a green salad.

TURKEY BREASTS CORDON BLEU

Preparation time: about 3 minutes
Cooking time: about 7½–9 minutes, plus grilling
Microwave setting: Maximum (Full)

4 turkey breasts, total
  weight 750 g (1½ lb)
freshly ground black
  pepper

50 g (2 oz) butter, diced
4 slices of cooked ham
4 slices of Gruyère cheese
parsley sprigs, to garnish

1. Place the turkey breasts in a shallow casserole
dish. Sprinkle with pepper and dot with the butter.
Cover and cook for 6 minutes, turning over and
rearranging the meat halfway through cooking.
2. Transfer to a serving plate. Place a slice of ham
and then cheese on top of each breast. Cook,
uncovered, for 3 minutes. **Brown under a preheated
conventional grill, if preferred.** Garnish with parsley.

CHICKEN & PEPPERS

Preparation time: about 20 minutes Cooking time: about 26½–29½ minutes
Microwave setting: Maximum (Full)

4 chicken pieces, total weight 1.25 kg (2½ lb)	1 teaspoon dried sage
1 carrot, peeled and sliced	1 teaspoon dried parsley
1 medium onion, peeled and sliced	2 tablespoons tomato purée
1 small red pepper, cored, seeded and sliced	25 g (1 oz) butter, cut into pieces
1 small green pepper, cored, seeded and sliced	25 g (1 oz) plain flour
	about 450 ml (¾ pint) hot chicken stock
1 garlic clove, peeled and crushed	salt
	freshly ground black pepper

1. Place the chicken pieces in a large bowl. Cover and cook for 9–12 minutes, rearranging halfway through cooking. Set aside, covered.
2. Place the carrot, onion, peppers, garlic, sage, parsley and tomato purée in a large bowl. Cover and cook for 10 minutes, stirring halfway through.
3. Stir in the butter until melted, then stir in the flour. Make up the chicken juices to 450 ml (¾ pint) with stock, then stir in with salt and pepper. Cook, uncovered, for 3½ minutes, stirring every minute.
4. Stir in the chicken and, cook, uncovered, for 4 minutes.
5. Serve with Duchesse potatoes.

CHICKEN LIVER & GRAPES

Preparation time: about 20 minutes Cooking time: about 16½ minutes
Microwave setting: Maximum (Full)

100 g (4 oz) butter	350 g (12 oz) black grapes, halved and seeded
1 garlic clove, peeled and crushed	salt
2 tablespoons tomato purée	freshly ground black pepper
1 tablespoon chopped fresh parsley	25 g (1 oz) cornflour
25 g (1 oz) mushrooms, finely sliced	125 ml (4 fl oz) red wine
750 g (1½ lb) chicken livers, chopped	chopped fresh parsley, to garnish

1. Place the butter, garlic, tomato purée, parsley and mushrooms in a large bowl. Cover and cook for 3 minutes.
2. Stir in the livers. Cover and cook for 6 minutes. Stir in the grapes, salt and pepper. Cover and cook for 5 minutes.
3. Blend together the cornflour and wine, then stir into the livers. Cook, uncovered, for 2½ minutes, stirring halfway through cooking.
4. Garnish with the chopped parsley and serve with rice and courgettes.

Clockwise: Chicken marengo;
Coq au vin; Chicken liver and
grapes; Chicken and peppers

CHICKEN MARENGO

Preparation time: about 15 minutes Cooking time: about 28 minutes
Microwave setting: maximum (Full)

1 onion, peeled and finely chopped	½ teaspoon dried rosemary
	½ teaspoon dried sage
4 chicken portions, total weight 1 kg (2 lb)	25 g (1 oz) butter, cut into pieces
6 tomatoes, skinned and chopped	25 g (1 oz) plain flour
175 g (6 oz) button mushrooms	about 150 ml (¼ pint) hot chicken stock
2 tablespoons tomato purée	150 ml (¼ pint) Marsala
	salt
1 garlic clove, peeled and crushed	freshly ground black pepper
	fresh sage, to garnish

1. Place the onion in a large bowl, cover and cook for 2 minutes. Add the chicken pieces, cover and cook for 10 minutes, rearranging halfway through cooking. Set aside, covered.
2. Place the tomatoes, mushrooms, tomato purée, garlic, rosemary and sage in a large bowl. Cover and cook for 8 minutes, stirring halfway through.
3. Stir in the butter until melted. Stir in the flour. Make up the chicken juices to 150 ml (¼ pint) with stock, then stir in with the Marsala, and salt and pepper. Cover and cook for 4 minutes, stirring halfway through.
4. Stir in the chicken and onions. Cook, uncovered, for 4 minutes. Garnish with sage.

COQ AU VIN

Preparation time: about 20 minutes Cooking time: about 50 minutes
Microwave setting: Maximum (Full) and Defrost

1 medium onion, peeled and finely chopped	600 ml (1 pint) red wine
100 g (4 oz) streaky bacon, rinds removed and chopped	2 garlic cloves, peeled and crushed
	25 g (1 oz) butter, cut into pieces
100 g (4 oz) button mushrooms	1 bouquet garni
1 × 1.5 kg (3 lb) chicken, cut into 8 pieces	1 tablespoon brandy (optional)
150 ml (¼ pint) hot chicken stock	salt
	freshly ground black pepper

This sauce is thin but can be thickened by blending about 40 g (1½ oz) cornflour with water to make a smooth paste. Remove the chicken, mix the paste into the sauce and bring back to the boil, 3–4 minutes.

1. Place the onion in a large bowl, cover and cook on Maximum for 4 minutes. Stir in the bacon and cook, uncovered, for 1 minute. Stir in the mushrooms and cook for 1 minute.
2. Stir in the chicken pieces and cook on Maximum, uncovered, for 8 minutes, stirring halfway through.
3. Stir in the stock, wine, garlic, butter, bouquet garni, brandy, if using, and salt and pepper to taste. Cook, covered, on Maximum for 6 minutes.
4. Using the Defrost setting, cook, covered, for 30 minutes. Halfway through cooking, remove the cover and stir.
5. Before serving, remove the bouquet garni.

SHERRY CHICKEN

Preparation time: about 10 minutes Cooking time: about 26–29 minutes
Microwave setting: Maximum (Full)

4 chicken legs, total weight
  1 kg (2 lb)
1 courgette, sliced
1 medium onion, peeled
  and sliced
½ teaspoon dried rosemary
1 teaspoon chopped fresh
  parsley
½ teaspoon dried tarragon
1 garlic clove, peeled and
  crushed
25 g (1 oz) butter, diced

25 g (1 oz) cornflour
about 300 ml (½ pint) hot
  chicken stock
150 ml (¼ pint) dry sherry
1 tablespoon tomato purée
50 g (2 oz) flaked almonds
salt
freshly ground black
  pepper
2 tablespoons double
  cream

1. Place the chicken legs in an oblong casserole.
Cover and cook for 9–12 minutes, rearranging
halfway through cooking. Set aside, covered.
2. Place the courgette, onion, rosemary, parsley,
tarragon and garlic in a large bowl. Cover and cook
for 5 minutes.
3. Stir in the butter until melted. Stir in the cornflour.
Make up the chicken juices to 300 ml (½ pint) with the
stock, then stir in with the sherry, tomato purée,
almonds, salt and pepper. Cook, uncovered, for 4
minutes, stirring every minute. Stir in the cream.
4. Pour over the chicken. Cook for 4 minutes.

TURKEY WITH ORANGE & ALMONDS

Preparation time: about 10 minutes Cooking time: about 10 minutes
Microwave setting: Maximum (Full)

4 turkey breasts, total
  weight 750 g (1½ lb)
freshly ground black
  pepper
grated rind of 1 orange
50 g (2 oz) flaked almonds,
  toasted
50 g (2 oz) butter

125 ml (4 fl oz) orange juice
1 tablespoon Grand
  Marnier
25 g (1 oz) soft dark brown
  sugar
1 orange, peeled and
  sliced, to garnish

1. Place the turkey breasts in a shallow casserole
dish and sprinkle with pepper. Cover and cook for 6
minutes. Rearrange and turn over halfway through
cooking. Set aside, covered.
2. Place the orange rind, almonds, butter, orange
juice, Grand Marnier and sugar in a jug. Cook,
uncovered, for 2 minutes.
3. Drain the juice off the breasts. Pour over the hot
sauce. Cook, uncovered, for 2 minutes. Garnish with
orange slices.

From left to right: Sherry
chicken; Turkey with orange and
almonds; Stuffed roast chicken;
Turkey legs casserole

STUFFED ROAST CHICKEN

Preparation time: about 20 minutes, plus soaking
Cooking time: about 27½ minutes, plus standing
Microwave setting: Maximum (Full)

1 celery stick, finely chopped
1 medium onion, peeled and finely chopped
1 eating apple, peeled, cored and chopped
175 g (6 oz) dried prunes, soaked in 125 ml (4 fl oz) port overnight, and chopped
1 × 1.5 kg (3 lb) roasting chicken
2 tablespoons clear honey
1 teaspoon Worcestershire sauce
1 teaspoon soy sauce
parsley sprigs, to garnish

1. Place the celery, onion and apple in a medium bowl. Cover. Cook for 3½ minutes. Stir in prunes.
2. Spoon stuffing into the chicken, and secure the opening and the legs with trussing thread.
3. Mix the honey, Worcestershire sauce and soy sauce together. Brush the chicken with the sauce.
4. Place the bird in a roasting bag. Secure with a non-metallic tie and prick the bag. Place the bird breast side down in a shallow dish. Cook for 12 minutes. Turn over and cook for a further 12 minutes.
5. Remove the chicken from the bag and wrap tightly in foil. Leave to stand for 15 minutes. Garnish with parsley sprigs.

TURKEY LEGS CASSEROLE

Preparation time: about 20 minutes Cooking time: about 29 minutes
Microwave setting: Maximum (Full)

4 turkey legs, total weight 1.25 kg (2½ lb)
1 celery stick, chopped
1 small turnip, peeled and diced
1 medium onion, peeled and chopped
1 carrot, peeled and sliced
1 tablespoon tomato purée
½ teaspoon dried marjoram
½ teaspoon dried thyme
1 teaspoon dried parsley
25 g (1 oz) butter, cut into pieces
25 g (1 oz) plain flour
about 450 ml (¾ pint) chicken stock
salt
freshly ground black pepper
chopped fresh parsley, to garnish

1. Place the turkey legs in a large bowl. Cover and cook for 12 minutes, rearranging halfway through cooking. Set aside, covered.
2. Place the celery, turnip, onion, carrot, tomato purée, marjoram, thyme and parsley in a large bowl. Cover and cook for 10 minutes, stirring halfway through cooking.
3. Stir in the butter until melted. Stir in the flour. Make up turkey juices to 450 ml (¾ pint) with stock, then stir in with salt and pepper. Cook, uncovered, for 3 minutes, stirring every minute.
4. Pour the vegetable sauce over the turkey. Cook, uncovered, for 4 minutes. Garnish with parsley.

CHICKEN IN SWEET & SOUR SAUCE

Preparation time: about 15 minutes Cooking time: about 24–27 minutes
Microwave setting: Maximum (Full)

4 chicken legs, total weight
   1.25 kg (2½ lb)
1 medium onion, peeled
   and chopped
½ green pepper, cored,
   seeded and diced
½ red pepper, cored,
   seeded and diced
1 teaspoon dried mixed
   herbs
1 garlic clove, peeled and
   crushed

25 g (1 oz) butter, diced
25 g (1 oz) plain flour
about 300 ml (½ pint) hot
   chicken stock
2 tablespoons white wine
   vinegar
1 tablespoon soy sauce
1 tablespoon marmalade
100 g (4 oz) dates, halved
   and stoned
50 g (2 oz) brown sugar
freshly ground pepper

1. Place chicken in bowl, cover and cook for 13 minutes, rearranging after 6. Set aside, covered.
2. Place the onion, peppers, herbs and garlic in a bowl, cover and cook for 4–6 minutes, stirring halfway through. Stir in butter, cover, cook for 2 minutes.
3. Stir in the flour. Make the chicken juices up to 300 ml (½ pint) with stock, then stir in with the remaining ingredients. Cover. Cook for 3 minutes, stirring halfway through.
4. Add the chicken, cover and cook for 3 minutes.

CHAUDFROID CHICKEN

Preparation time: about 50 minutes, plus chilling
Cooking time: about 11 minutes Microwave setting: Maximum (Full)

1 piece of carrot
1 celery stick, halved
1 small onion, peeled and
   stuck with 8 black
   peppercorns
1 bay leaf
600 ml (1 pint) milk
600 ml (1 pint) cold water
25 g (1 oz) aspic jelly
   powder
50 g (2 oz) butter
50 g (2 oz) plain flour
1 teaspoon powdered
   gelatine
2 tablespoons double
   cream

salt
freshly ground white
   pepper
4 chicken legs, total weight
   1 kg (2 lb), cooked and
   skinned

To garnish:
4 long, thin strips of green
   pepper skin, to
   resemble flower stems
16 pieces of red pepper
   skin, cut into petal
   shapes
12 pieces of green pepper
   skin, cut into leaf shapes

1. Place the carrot, celery, onion, bay leaf and milk in a large jug. Cook, uncovered, for 4 minutes. Set aside for 15 minutes to infuse.
2. Meanwhile, place half of the cold water in a jug and cook, uncovered, for 3½ minutes. Stir in the aspic jelly powder until dissolved, then stir in the remaining cold water. Stand the jug in a bowl of hot water.

3. Place the butter in a large jug and cook, uncovered, for 1 minute or until melted. Blend in the flour, then gradually stir in the strained flavoured milk. Cook, uncovered, for $2\frac{1}{2}$ minutes, stirring every minute.
4. Stir the gelatine into 150 ml ($\frac{1}{4}$ pint) of the aspic jelly until dissolved. Beat this mixture into the sauce with the cream and salt and pepper to taste. Continue beating until smooth and glossy.
5. Place the chicken legs on a wire tray over a tray. Using a spoon, gently coat the chicken legs with the sauce. Continue coating the legs until completely covered.
6. Allow the sauce to set slightly before decorating, then garnish the legs with the pepper skin pieces to represent flowers.
7. Using a spoon, slowly and gently coat the legs with 2 or 3 layers of the remaining aspic jelly. Chill until set.
8. Pour the remaining aspic jelly into a shallow tray and chill until set.
9. Using a knife, cut the jelly into small squares. Serve the chicken surround by diced jelly.

CHICKEN À LA KING

Preparation time: about 15 minutes Cooking time: about 14½ minutes
Microwave setting: Maximum (Full)

100 g (4 oz) diced green pepper
100 g (4 oz) frozen peas
100 g (4 oz) butter, cut into small pieces
100 g (4 oz) plain flour
750 ml (1¼ pints) hot chicken stock
450 g (1 lb) cooked chicken meat, diced
salt
freshly ground black pepper

To garnish:
4 slices of white bread, cut into triangles and fried
chopped fresh parsley

1. Place the green pepper in a medium bowl, cover and cook for 3 minutes. Stir in the peas, cover and cook for 3 minutes.
2. Stir in the butter until melted. Stir in the flour and cook for 30 seconds. Slowly blend in the stock. Stir in the chicken, and salt and pepper to taste. Cook, uncovered, for 8 minutes, stirring every minute.
3. Arrange with bread triangles, garnish with parsley.

From left to right: Chicken in sweet and sour sauce; Chaudfroid chicken; Chicken à la king

TURKEY CASSEROLE

Preparation time: about 15 minutes Cooking time: about 18½ minutes
Microwave setting: Maximum (Full)

4 turkey fillets
1 carrot, peeled and finely sliced
1 celery stick, finely sliced
1 medium onion, peeled and finely chopped
50 g (2 oz) button mushrooms, finely sliced

40 g (1½ oz) butter
40 g (1½ oz) plain flour
150 ml (¼ pint) sherry
450 ml (¾ pint) hot chicken stock
salt
freshly ground black pepper

1. Place the turkey fillets in a large shallow casserole. Cover and cook for 2 minutes.
2. Turn the casserole round and cook for a further 2 minutes. Turn the casserole round again and cook for 1½ minutes. Set aside.
3. Place the carrot, celery, onion, mushrooms and butter in a medium bowl. Cover and cook for 6 minutes, stirring halfway through cooking.
4. Stir in the flour, sherry, hot stock, salt and pepper. Cover and cook for 2 minutes, stirring halfway through.
5. Pour over the turkey. Cover. Cook for 5 minutes.

CHICKEN IN VERMOUTH

Preparation time: about 15 minutes Cooking time: about 26 minutes
Microwave setting: Maximum (Full)

1 medium onion, peeled and finely chopped
½ green pepper, cored, seeded and finely chopped
100 g (4 oz) mushrooms, sliced
1 teaspoon dried basil
50 g (2 oz) butter
salt

freshly ground black pepper
4 chicken quarters
50 g (2 oz) cornflour
150 ml (¼ pint) dry white vermouth
300 ml (½ pint) milk
300 ml (½ pint) hot chicken stock
flat-leaved parsley sprigs, to garnish

1. Place the onion and green pepper in a large bowl. Cover and cook for 4 minutes. Stir in the mushrooms, basil, butter, salt and pepper.
2. Arrange the chicken around the sides of the bowl, cover and cook for 8 minutes.
3. Stir the chicken and vegetables together and turn the bowl round. Cook for a further 7 minutes. Remove the chicken from the bowl and set aside.
4. Blend the cornflour and vermouth together, then

gradually stir in the milk. Add to the vegetables. Stir in the hot stock. Cool slightly.

5. Pour into a liquidizer and blend until smooth. Pour the sauce back into the bowl, cover and cook for 2 minutes.

6. Return the chicken to the bowl, cover and cook for 5 minutes. Garnish with sprigs of parsley and serve.

GLAZED POUSSINS

Preparation time: about 10 minutes Cooking time: about 33 minutes
Microwave setting: Maximum (Full)

25 g (1 oz) butter
1 tablespoon soft dark
  brown sugar
1 tablespoon
  Worcestershire sauce
4 bacon rashers, rinds
  removed

4 poussins, total weight 1.5
  kg (3lb), trussed
watercress sprigs, to
  garnish

1. Place the butter, sugar and Worcestershire sauce in a small jug. Cook, uncovered, for 1 minute. Set aside.

2. Push a rasher of bacon into each chicken. Place the chickens, breast side down, in a shallow casserole. Cook, uncovered, for 12 minutes. Turn the chickens over and brush with the sugar glaze. Cook, uncovered, for 10 minutes. Wrap the casserole in foil and leave to stand, covered, for 10 minutes. Garnish with watercress and serve.

From left to right: Turkey
casserole; Chicken in vermouth;
Glazed poussins

BRAISED PIGEONS

Preparation time: about 10 minutes
Cooking time: about 29 minutes, plus standing
Microwave setting: Maximum (Full)

4 bacon rashers, rinds
  removed, then rolled
4 pigeons, drawn and
  trussed, total weight 1.25
  kg (2½ lb)
2 small onions, peeled and
  sliced
50 g (2 oz) mushrooms,
  sliced
1 tablespoon tomato purée
¼ teaspoon dried thyme
¼ teaspoon dried parsley

¼ teaspoon dried rosemary
¼ teaspoon dried marjoram
1 garlic clove, peeled and
  crushed
25 g (1 oz) butter, diced
25 g (1 oz) plain flour
300 ml (½ pint) hot chicken
  stock
300 ml (½ pint) red wine
salt
freshly ground black
  pepper

1. Place a bacon rasher inside each pigeon. Place the pigeons in a 23 cm (9 inch) round, shallow casserole dish, breast side down. Cover and cook for 8 minutes. Turn pigeons over and cook, uncovered, for 5 minutes. Set aside, covered.
2. Place the onions, mushrooms, tomato purée, herbs and garlic in a medium bowl. Cover and cook for 6 minutes, stirring halfway through cooking.
3. Stir in the butter until melted. Stir in the flour, stock, wine, and salt and pepper to taste. Cook, uncovered, for 4 minutes, stirring every minute.
4. Pour the sauce over the pigeons. Cover and cook for 6 minutes. Stand, covered, for 5 minutes.

ROAST PHEASANT WITH BREAD SAUCE

Preparation time, about 15 minutes
Cooking time: about 23 minutes, plus standing and grilling
Microwave setting: Maximum (Full)

1 medium onion, peeled
6 cloves
150 ml (¼ pint) milk
150 ml (¼ pint) cold chicken
  stock
100 g (4 oz) fresh white
  breadcrumbs
75 g (3 oz) butter

salt
freshly ground black
  pepper
1 × 1 kg (2 lb) pheasant
3 streaky bacon rashers,
  rinds removed
1 tablespoon plain flour

1. To make the sauce, stud the onion with the cloves and place in a medium bowl. Add the milk, chicken stock, breadcrumbs, 50 g (2 oz) of the butter, salt and pepper. Cook for 5½ minutes, stirring halfway.
2. Place the remaining butter inside the pheasant and secure the opening with trussing thread. Lay the bacon over the breast and secure.
3. Place the pheasant in a roasting bag, and secure with a non-metallic tie. Prick the bag and place in a shallow casserole. Cook for 7 minutes. Turn the pheasant over and cook for a further 7 minutes.
4. Remove the pheasant from the bag and discard the bacon. Wrap in foil. Stand for 10 minutes.
5. Place the pheasant in a grill pan. Sprinkle with flour and **brown under a preheated conventional grill.**
6. Meanwhile, remove and discard the onion from the sauce. Cook for 3½ minutes, stirring halfway.

RABBIT IN WHITE WINE

Preparation time: about 20 minutes
Coking time: about 19 minutes, plus standing
Microwave setting: Maximum (Full)

1 medium onion, peeled
  and finely chopped
1 celery stick, finely sliced
1 carrot, peeled and finely
  diced
½ green pepper, cored,
  seeded and finely diced
1 garlic clove, peeled and
  crushed
½ teaspoon dried rosemary
1 teaspoon chopped fresh
  parsley

50 g (2 oz) butter
4 rabbit joints
50 g (2 oz) cornflour
300 ml (½ pint) hot chicken
  stock
150 ml (¼ pint) milk
150 ml (¼ pint) white wine
salt
freshly ground black
  pepper
rosemary sprigs, to
  garnish

1. Place the onion, celery, carrot, green pepper, garlic, rosemary, parsley and butter in a large bowl. Cover and cook for 9 minutes, stirring halfway through cooking.
2. Place the rabbit around the sides of the bowl. Cover and cook for 3 minutes.
3. Stir the rabbit and vegetables together and turn the bowl round. Cook for a further 3 minutes.
4. Remove the rabbit. Stir in the cornflour, then blend in the hot stock, milk, wine, salt and pepper.
5. Return the rabbit to the bowl, cover and cook for 4 minutes. Leave to stand, covered, for 5 minutes before serving, garnished with rosemary.

DUCK WITH RED WINE SAUCE

Preparation time: about 20 minutes
Cooking time: 32 minutes, plus grilling Microwave setting: Maximum (Full)

4 duck joints
3 tomatoes
1 medium onion, peeled
  and finely chopped
50 g (2 oz) butter
2 tablespoons tomato
  purée
2 garlic cloves, peeled and
  crushed

½ teaspoon dried rosemary
½ teaspoon dried basil
salt
freshly ground black
  pepper
50 g (2 oz) cornflour
150 ml (¼ pint) dry red wine
450 ml (¾ pint) hot chicken
  stock

1. Place the pieces of duck in a large bowl. Cover and cook for 8 minutes. turn the bowl round and cook for a further 7 minutes.
2. Place the joints in a grill pan and **brown under a preheated conventional grill.** Keep hot.
3. Meanwhile, skin the tomatoes by pricking them with a fork and placing in a large bowl. Cover with 600 ml (1 pint) cold water and cook for 6 minutes. Drain immediately to prevent the tomatoes cooking and remove the skins with a knife. Chop the flesh.
4. Place the onion, butter, tomatoes, tomato purée, garlic, rosemary, basil, salt and pepper in a large bowl. Cover and cook for 8 minutes.
5. Blend the cornflour and wine together. Stir the cornflour mixture into the vegetables, then stir in the hot stock. Cool slightly.
6. Pour into a liquidizer and blend until smooth.
7. Pour into a large bowl and cook for 3 minutes or until thickened and hot, stirring halfway through.

Clockwise: Rabbit in white wine; Duck with red wine sauce; Roast pheasant with bread sauce: Braised pigeons

ROAST DUCK

Preparation time: about 5 minutes
Cooking time: about 40 minutes, plus standing and grilling
Microwave setting: Maximum (Full)

1 × 2.75 kg (6 lb) duck, washed and cleaned
1 orange, cut into 8 pieces

1. Stuff the duck with the orange pieces. Truss with string. Place in a roasting bag and tie the opening with string. Pierce the bag.
2. Place the bird, breast side down, on a trivet in a shallow container. Cook for 20 minutes.
3. Drain off the fat and juices. Remove the bag and return to the cooker with the breast side up. Cook uncovered for 20 minutes.
4. Wrap the bird in foil and stand for 15 minutes.
5. **Brown under a preheated conventional grill**, in portions if necessary.

SPICED DUCK

Preparation time: about 5 minutes, plus marinating overnight
Cooking time: about 23½ minutes, plus standing and grilling
Microwave setting: Maximum (Full)

1 large onion, peeled and chopped	4 tablespoons lemon juice
3 tablespoons dark soft brown sugar	½ teaspoon dried rosemary
1½ teaspoons salt	½ teaspoon dried chives
2 tablespoons paprika	½ teaspoon grated nutmeg
2 tablespoons tomato purée	900 ml (1½ pints) cold water
2 tablespoons Worcestershire sauce	freshly ground black pepper
4 tablespoons white wine vinegar	1 × 2 kg (4½ lb) duck, quartered
	25 g (1 oz) butter
	25 g (1 oz) plain flour
	spring onions, to garnish

1. Place the onion, sugar, salt, paprika, tomato purée, Worcestershire sauce, vinegar, lemon juice, rosemary, chives, nutmeg, water, and pepper to taste in a large bowl. Add the duck and leave to marinate overnight.
2. Drain the duck, reserving the marinade. Place in a large bowl, cover and cook for 10 minutes. Halfway through cooking, drain off the juice, then rearrange the duck pieces.
3. Leave the duck to stand, covered, for 10 minutes. Drain off the juices and cook, covered, for a further 8 minutes.
4. Place the duck on a grill pan and **grill under a preheated conventional grill** until the skin is crisp.
5. Meanwhile, place the butter in a large jug and cook, uncovered, for 30 seconds or until melted. Stir in the flour. Measure out 600 ml (1 pint) of the strained reserved marinade. Blend into the butter and flour mixture. Cook, uncovered, for 5 minutes, stirring every minute.
6. Serve the duck with the sauce, garnished with spring onions.

Roast duck; Spiced duck

STUFFED ROAST TURKEY

Preparation time: about 15 minutes
Cooking time: about 58 minutes, plus standing
Microwave setting: Maximum (Full)

25 g (1 oz) butter
1 large onion, peeled and
  finely chopped
50 g (2 oz) fresh white
  breadcrumbs
50 g (2 oz) fresh brown
  breadcrumbs
150 ml ($\frac{1}{4}$ pint) hot chicken
  stock
$\frac{1}{4}$ teaspoon dried thyme
$\frac{1}{4}$ teaspoon dried rosemary
$\frac{1}{4}$ teaspoon dried marjoram
1 teaspoon dried parsley
$\frac{1}{4}$ teaspoon dried sage
1 orange, peeled and
  chopped

grated rind of 1 orange
25 g (1 oz) sultanas
salt
freshly ground black
  pepper
1 × 3 kg (7 lb) turkey,
  thawed if frozen and at
  room temperature
watercress, to garnish

Glaze:
50 g (2 oz) butter
2 tablespoons soft dark
  brown sugar
$\frac{1}{2}$ tablespoon sherry
2 teaspoons soy sauce

If using a different size of turkey, allow $7\frac{1}{2}$ minutes to each 450 g (1 lb) for turkeys under 4.5 kg (10 lb) in weight.

1. Place the butter and onion in a medium bowl, cover and cook for 4 minutes. Stir in the breadcrumbs, stock, thyme, rosemary, marjoram, parsley, sage, orange, orange rind, sultanas, and salt and pepper to taste. Stuff and truss the turkey.
2. If recommended (see page 8), mask wings and legs with pieces of foil. Place the turkey, breast side down, on an inverted plate in a shallow dish. Cover with a paper towel. Cook for $26\frac{1}{4}$ minutes. Set aside.
3. Place the butter, sugar, sherry and soy sauce in a small jug. Cook for $1\frac{1}{2}$ minutes.

4. Remove the foil pieces from the turkey, turn over and brush with the glaze. Cook for $26\frac{1}{4}$ minutes.
5. Wrap in foil and stand for 30 minutes.
6. Garnish with watercress and serve with sauces, gravy and vegetables.

CHRISTMAS LUNCH

Honeyed Grapefruit and Orange

Roast Turkey
Cranberry Sauce
Peas
Potatoes, or roast potatoes
Gravy
Bread Sauce

Christmas Pudding

Order of Cooking:
1. Earlier in the day, prepare the starter ingredients (page 24), stuff the turkey, prepare the potatoes (page 105), make the cranberry and bread sauces (page 140), and mix the Christmas Pudding (page 121).
2. Cook the turkey, and while standing, cook the potatoes. During the potato standing time, cook the peas, make the gravy and reheat the bread sauce for about 3 minutes.
3. Cook the pudding while serving the main course.

Honeyed grapefruit and orange; Christmas pudding; Bread sauce;
Peas; Roast turkey; Potatoes; Gravy; Cranberry sauce

Fish pie; Fish risotto

FISH

FISH RISOTTO

Preparation time: about 15 minutes
Cooking time: about 30 minutes, plus standing
Microwave setting: Maximum (Full)

50 g (2 oz) butter
1 large onion, peeled and
  finely chopped
½ green pepper, cored,
  seeded and finely diced
½ red pepper, cored,
  seeded and finely diced
2 tablespoons tomato
  purée
1 garlic clove, peeled and
  crushed
1 teaspoon dried mixed
  herbs

50 g (2 oz) mushrooms,
  finely chopped
350 g (12 oz) long-grain
  rice
750 ml (1¼ pints) hot
  chicken stock
salt
¼ teaspoon oil
750 g (1½ lb) cod fillets,
  rinsed in cold water
freshly ground black
  pepper

1. Place the butter, onion, peppers, tomato purée,
garlic, herbs and mushrooms in a large bowl. Cover
and cook for 10 minutes, stirring halfway through.
2. Stir in the rice, stock, salt and oil. Cover and cook
for 13 minutes. Stir halfway through cooking. Set
aside, covered.
3. Place the fillets in a shallow dish. Cover and cook
for 7 minutes, rearranging halfway through cooking.
Leave to stand for 4 minutes, covered.
4. Flake the fish, removing any skin. Stir the fish into
the rice mixture and season to taste with pepper.

FISH PIE

Preparation time: about 10 minutes Cooking time: about 23½ minutes
Microwave setting: Maximum (Full)

450 g (1 lb) smoked
  haddock fillets
3 tablespoons water
salt
750 g (1½ lb) potatoes,
  peeled and cubed
about 4 tablespoons milk
15 g (½ oz) butter
freshly ground black
  pepper

Sauce:
25 g (1 oz) butter
25 g (1 oz) plain flour
salt
freshly ground black
  pepper
1 hard-boiled egg, finely
  chopped
parsley sprigs, to garnish

If using frozen haddock fillets, cook for a further 3
minutes at step 1.
1. Place the fish in a large bowl. Cover and cook for
6 minutes, rearranging halfway through cooking.
Set aside, covered.
2. Place the water, salt and potatoes in a large bowl.
Cover and cook for 10 minutes. Set aside, covered.
3. Drain the liquid from the fish and make up to
300 ml (½ pint) with milk.
4. To make the sauce, place the butter in a large jug
and cook for 30 seconds. Stir in the flour, milk/fish
liquid, and salt and pepper to taste. Cook for 3
minutes, stirring every minute.
5. Flake the fish, removing any skin and bones. Fold
into the sauce with the chopped egg.
6. Mash the potatoes with the butter, remaining milk
and pepper to taste.
7. Pour the fish mixture into a 1.2 litre (2 pint)
casserole dish. Pipe the potatoes over the fish. Cook,
uncovered, for 4 minutes. Garnish with sprigs of
parsley, and serve with peas.

STEAMED FISH

Preparation time: about 3 minutes
Cooking time: about 6 minutes, plus standing
Microwave setting: Maximum (Full)

450 g (1 lb) fresh white fish
  (e.g. haddock, cod)

To garnish:
lemon slices
parsley sprigs

The addition of water is unnecessary in this recipe.
1. Place the fish in a shallow dish. Cover and cook for 6 minutes.
2. Leave to stand, covered, for 3–4 minutes or until the fish is opaque and the flesh flakes easily when tested with a fork. Serve garnished with lemon slices and parsley sprigs.

From left to right: Steamed fish;
Cod with herbs; Stuffed trout;
Mackerel roll-ups

COD WITH HERBS

Preparation time: about 10 minutes
Cooking time: about 9½ minutes, plus standing
Microwave setting: Maximum (Full)

1 small onion, peeled and
  chopped
½ teaspoon dried thyme
½ teaspoon dried parsley
½ teaspoon dried rosemary
½ teaspoon dried sage
50 g (2 oz) fresh white
  breadcrumbs

3 tablespoons water
salt
freshly ground black
  pepper
4 cod steaks, total weight
  750 g (1½ lb)
25 g (1 oz) butter, cut into
  pieces

1. Place the onion in a medium bowl, cover and cook for 2½ minutes. Stir in the thyme, parsley, rosemary, sage, breadcrumbs, water, and salt and pepper to taste. Set aside.
2. Place the cod steaks, thin ends to the centre, in a shallow casserole. Cover and cook for 4 minutes.
3. Stuff each steak with the herb mixture. Sprinkle with pepper, and dot with the butter. Cover and cook for 3 minutes. Leave to stand, covered, for 3 minutes before serving.
4. Serve with green noodles and Cauliflower cheese (page 102).

STUFFED TROUT

Preparation time: about 15 minutes
Cooking time: about 12 minutes, plus standing
Microwave setting: Maximum (Full)

25 g (1 oz) flaked almonds
100 g (4 oz) cooked peeled
    prawns
4 tablespoons fresh white
    breadcrumbs
2 tablespoons lemon juice
salt
freshly ground black
    pepper

4 trout, total weight 1 kg (2¼
    lb), cleaned, with heads
    left on

To garnish:
parsley sprigs
lemon twists

1. Mix together the almonds, prawns, breadcrumbs,
lemon juice, and plenty of salt and pepper to taste.
2. Fill each trout with the stuffing. Cover and cook for
12 minutes, rearranging halfway through cooking.
Leave to stand, covered, for 5 minutes before
serving.
3. Garnish with parsley and lemon twists.

MACKEREL ROLL-UPS

Preparation time: about 15 minutes
Cooking time: about 11 minutes, plus standing
Microwave setting: Maximum (Full)

75 g (3 oz) fresh brown
    breadcrumbs
½ teaspoon dried marjoram
½ teaspoon dried thyme
½ teaspoon dried parsley
½ teaspoon dried sage
grated rind of 1 lemon
2 tablespoons lemon juice
1 teaspoon anchovy
    essence
6 tablespoons hot water

salt
freshly ground black
    pepper
4 mackerel, about 350 g
    (12 oz) each, cleaned and
    filleted

To garnish:
lemon slices
parsley sprigs

1. Mix together the breadcrumbs, marjoram, thyme,
parsley, sage, lemon rind, lemon juice, anchovy
essence, water, and salt and pepper to taste.
2. Spread the stuffing over the fish. Roll up from the
head to the tail. Secure with wooden cocktail sticks.
Cover and cook for 11 minutes, rearranging halfway
through cooking.
3. Leave to stand, covered, for 5 minutes before
serving, garnished with lemon slices and parsley.

HERRINGS WITH MUSTARD SAUCE

Preparation time: about 15 minutes Cooking time: about 12–14 minutes
Microwave setting: Maximum (Full)

1 small onion, peeled and chopped	**Sauce:**
½ teaspoon dried thyme	40 g (1½ oz) butter
½ teaspoon dried marjoram	25 g (1 oz) plain flour
grated rind of ½ lemon	450 ml (¾ pint) milk
50 g (2 oz) fresh brown breadcrumbs	1 tablespoon dry English mustard
salt	1 tablespoon white wine vinegar
freshly ground black pepper	1 teaspoon caster sugar
1 egg (size 4)	salt
4 herrings, total weight 350 g (12 oz), cleaned and gutted	freshly ground black pepper
	chopped parsley, to garnish

1. Place the onion in a small bowl, cover and cook for 3 minutes. Stir in the thyme, marjoram, lemon rind, breadcrumbs, salt and pepper and bind with egg.
2. Fill the herrings with the stuffing. Close and secure with wooden cocktail sticks. Place the herrings in a shallow casserole dish, cover and cook for 5 minutes, rearranging halfway through cooking. Set aside, covered, whilst making the sauce.
3. Place the butter in a large jug and cook for 1 minute or until melted. Stir in the flour. Gradually blend in the milk, mustard, vinegar, sugar and salt and pepper to taste. Cook for 4–6 minutes, stirring every minute.
4. Remove the cocktail sticks from the herrings and pour over the sauce. Sprinkle with chopped parsley to garnish and serve with new potatoes.

CHEESY SMOKED HADDOCK

Preparation time: about 5 minutes Cooking time: about 11 minutes
Microwave setting: Maximum (Full)

4 smoked haddock fillets, about 150 g (5 oz) each	1 teaspoon prepared mustard
25 g (1 oz) butter, cut into pieces	salt
	freshly ground black pepper
Cheese sauce:	50 g (2 oz) Cheddar cheese, grated
25 g (1 oz) butter	flat-leaved parsley, to garnish
25 g (1 oz) plain flour	
300 ml (½ pint) milk	

1. Place the fillets in a shallow casserole dish. Dot with the butter. Cover and cook for 6 minutes, rearranging halfway through cooking. Set aside, covered, whilst making the sauce.
2. Place the butter in a large jug and cook for 1 minute or until melted. Blend in the flour. Stir in the milk, mustard and salt and pepper. Cook, uncovered, for 3 minutes, stirring every minute.
3. Stir in the cheese and cook, uncovered, for 1 minute.
4. Drain the fish and arrange on a serving dish. Pour over the sauce. Garnish with sprigs of parsley.

BAKED HADDOCK CUTLETS WITH CAPERS

Preparation time: about 10 minutes Cooking time: about 16 minutes
Microwave setting: Maximum (Full)

25 g (1 oz) butter	salt
4 haddock cutlets	freshly ground black pepper
Sauce:	2 tablespoons capers, drained and chopped
25 g (1 oz) butter	1 tablespoon caper juice
25 g (1 oz) cornflour	dill sprigs, to garnish
300 ml (½ pint) milk	

1. Place the butter in a small dish. Cook for 1 minute or until melted.
2. Brush the haddock with the butter. Arrange the haddock in a shallow casserole, cover and cook for 4 minutes.
3. Turn the casserole round and cook for a further 4 minutes. Set aside, covered.
4. To make the sauce, place the butter in a 600 ml (1 pint) jug. Cook for 1 minute or until melted. Stir in the cornflour, and blend in the milk, salt and pepper. Cook for 4 minutes, stirring every minute.
5. Stir in the capers and their juice and pour the sauce over the fish. Cook for 2 minutes. Garnish with dill and serve.

FILLETS OF PLAICE IN WHITE WINE

Preparation time: about 15 minutes Cooking time: about 21 minutes
Microwave setting: Maximum (Full)

50 g (2 oz) button mushrooms, finely sliced	salt
1 medium onion, peeled and finely chopped	freshly ground black pepper
100 g (4 oz) butter	100 g (4 oz) white grapes, peeled, halved and seeded
300 ml (½ pint) dry white wine	
1 kg (2 lb) plaice fillets	**To garnish:**
50 g (2 oz) plain flour	4 lemon slices
300 ml (½ pint) milk	

1. Place the mushrooms, onion, 50 g (2 oz) of the butter and wine into a shallow casserole. Cover and cook for 4 minutes or until the onion is translucent.
2. Roll up the plaice fillets and place them in the casserole. Cover and cook for 4 minutes. Turn the casserole round and cook for a further 5 minutes.
3. Drain the fish, reserving the liquid and keep hot.
4. Place the remaining butter in 1 litre (1¾ pint) jug. Cook for 1 minute or until the butter has melted.
5. Blend in the flour, fish liquid, milk, salt and pepper. Cook for 7½ minutes, stirring every minute.
6. Stir in the grapes. Pour the sauce over the fish, cover and cook for 1 minute. Garnish with lemon.

Clockwise: Herrings with mustard sauce; Baked haddock cutlets with capers; Fillets of plaice in white wine; Cheesy smoked haddock

COD WITH ANCHOVIES

Preparation time: about 5 minutes Cooking time: about 7 minutes
Microwave setting: Maximum (Full)

4 cod steaks, total weight
  750 g (1½ lb)
salt
freshly ground black
  pepper
25 g (1 oz) butter, cut into 4
  pieces

1 × 40 g (1½ oz) can anchovy
  fillets, drained
16 capers

To garnish:
lemon slices
parsley sprigs

1. Place the cod steaks, with the thin ends to the centre, in a dish. Cover and cook for 4 minutes.
2. Season the steaks with salt and pepper and turn over. Place a piece of butter on each. Cover and cook for 1½ minutes.
3. Baste the fish with the melted butter. Arrange a cross of 2 anchovies on each steak with a caper in between. Cook, uncovered, for 1½ minutes. Garnish with lemon slices and parsley.

From left to right: Cod with
anchovies; Plaice fillets with
sweetcorn; Sole & shrimp rolls;
Spiced haddock

PLAICE FILLETS WITH SWEETCORN

Preparation time: about 10 minutes Cooking time: about 8½ minutes
Microwave setting: Maximum (Full)

12 skinned plaice fillets,
  total weight 600 g (1¼ lb)
75 g (3 oz) butter, cut into
  pieces
1 × 350 g (12 oz) can
  sweetcorn with sweet
  peppers, drained

salt
freshly ground black
  pepper
parsley sprigs, to garnish

1. Roll up the fillets and place in a shallow casserole dish. Cover and cook for 3½ minutes. Set aside, covered.
2. Place the butter in a jug and cook, uncovered, for 1 minute or until melted.
3. Place the butter, sweetcorn, and salt and pepper to taste in a blender. Blend until smooth.
4. Rearrange the fillets. Sprinkle with salt and pepper to taste, and spoon the sweetcorn mixture over the top.
5. Cook, uncovered, for 4 minutes.
6. Garnish with sprigs of parsley and serve immediately.

SOLE & SHRIMP ROLLS

Preparation time: about 16 minutes Cooking time: about 6 minutes
Microwave setting: Maximum (Full)

1 × 200 g (7 oz) can
   shrimps, drained or
   frozen shrimps, thawed
juice of ½ lemon
12–16 skinned sole fillets,
   total weight 750 g (1½ lb)
2 tablespoons dried
   parsley

salt
freshly ground black
   pepper
50 g (2 oz) butter, cut into
   pieces
chopped parsley, to
   garnish

1. Sprinkle the shrimps with lemon juice, then
spread over the fillets. Sprinkle over the dried
parsley, salt and pepper. Roll up and secure with
sticks.
2. Place the fish rolls in a shallow casserole dish.
Cover and cook for 4 minutes.
3. Rearrange. Dot the fish rolls with the butter.
Cover and cook for 2 minutes.
4. Remove the cocktail sticks. Garnish with chopped
parsley, and serve with duchesse potatoes and fried
courgettes or green beans.

SPICED HADDOCK

Preparation time: about 10 minutes Cooking time: about 10 minutes
Microwave setting: Maximum (Full)

1 small onion, peeled and
   chopped
600 g (1¼ lb) skinned
   haddock fillet, cut into
   pieces
50 g (2 oz) button
   mushrooms, sliced
1 garlic clove, peeled and
   crushed
2 tablespoons
   Worcestershire sauce

1 teaspoon dried mixed
   herbs
½ teaspoon curry powder
1 teaspoon soy sauce
1 × 400 g (14 oz) can
   tomatoes, chopped with
   their juice
salt
freshly ground black
   pepper

1. Place the onion in a large bowl, cover and cook
for 2½ minutes.
2. Stir in the haddock, mushrooms, garlic,
Worcestershire sauce, herbs, curry powder and
soy sauce. Cover and cook for 3½–4 minutes, stirring
halfway through cooking.
3. Stir in the tomatoes, and salt and pepper to taste.
Cook, uncovered, for 3½ minutes.
4. Serve surrounded by boiled rice with peas.

HADDOCK STEAKS WITH CARROTS

Preparation time: about 15 minutes Cooking time: about 17 minutes
Microwave setting: Maximum (Full)

1 medium onion, peeled
  and finely chopped
225 g (8 oz) carrots, peeled
  and finely grated
4 haddock steaks, total
  weight 750 g (1½ lb)

50 g (2 oz) butter
salt
freshly ground black
  pepper
parsley sprigs, to garnish

1. Place the onion in a medium bowl, cover and cook for 2 minutes. Stir in the carrots, cover and cook for 5 minutes. Set aside, covered.
2. Place the haddock steaks, with the thin ends to the centre, in a shallow casserole dish, cover and cook for 6 minutes. Set aside.
3. Place the butter in a small jug and cook, uncovered, for 1 minute or until melted. Stir the butter into the vegetables, and season to taste with salt and pepper. Stir in the liquid from the fish.
4. Top the fish steaks with the carrot mixture and pour over any juice. Cook, uncovered, for 3 minutes.
5. Garnish with the parsley sprigs.

LEMON TROUT

Preparation time: about 10 minutes
Cooking time: about 9 minutes, plus standing
Microwave setting: Maximum (Full)

1 lemon, cut into 8 wedges
4 trout, total weight 1 kg
  (2 lb), cleaned, with
  heads left on
grated rind of 2 lemons
50 g (2 oz) butter, cut into 8
  pieces

To garnish:
4 lemon twists
parsley sprigs

1. Place 2 wedges of lemon inside each trout. Place in a shallow casserole dish. Cover and cook for 4 minutes.
2. Rearrange the trout. Sprinkle with the lemon rind and dot with the butter. Cover and cook for 5 minutes. Halfway through cooking, baste the trout with the melted butter.
3. Leave to stand, covered, for 3 minutes.
4. Garnish with lemon twists and parsley, and serve with a mixed green salad.

Haddock steaks with carrots;
Lemon trout; Cod in tomato and
onion sauce; Mackerel in a bag

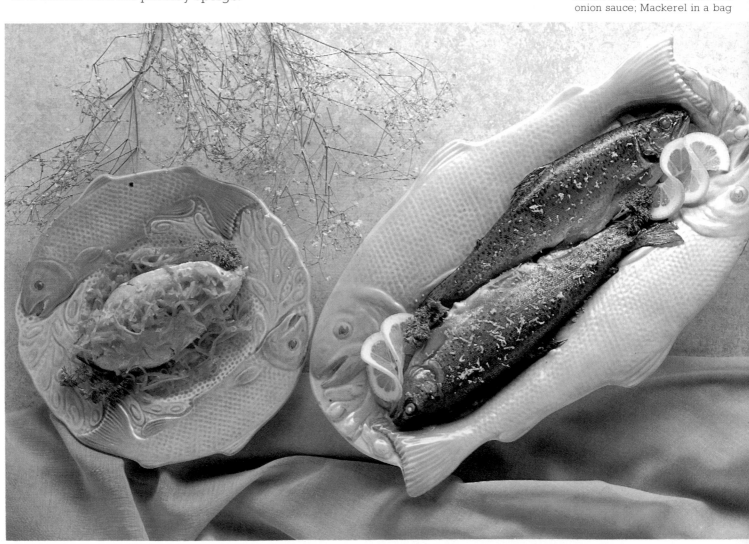

COD IN TOMATO & ONION SAUCE

Preparation time: about 10 minutes Cooking time: about 14 minutes
Microwave setting: Maximum (Full)

1 medium onion, peeled and finely sliced	½ teaspoon dried rosemary
4 tomatoes, skinned and chopped	1 garlic clove, peeled and crushed
1 tablespoon tomato purée	25 g (1 oz) butter
½ teaspoon dried thyme	salt
1 teaspoon chopped fresh parsley	freshly ground black pepper
½ teaspoon dried marjoram	4 cod steaks
	fresh dill, to garnish

1. Place the onion, tomatoes, tomato purée, thyme, parsley, marjoram, rosemary, garlic, butter, salt and pepper in a large bowl. Cover and cook for 6 minutes, stirring halfway through cooking. Set aside, covered while cooking the fish.
2. Place the fish in a shallow dish. Cover and cook for 3 minutes. Turn the dish round and cook for a further 3 minutes.
3. Pour the sauce over the fish. Cover and cook for 2 minutes, then garnish with dill.
4. Serve with creamed potatoes and green beans.

MACKEREL IN A BAG

Preparation time: about 10 minutes
Cooking time: about 12 minutes, plus standing
Microwave setting: Maximum (Full)

50 g (2 oz) butter	salt
4 mackerel, total weight 1.5 kg (3 lb), gutted	freshly ground black pepper
1 tablespoon chopped fresh parsley	lemon quarters and parsley sprigs, to garnish

1. Spread the butter inside each of the fish. Sprinkle the parsley over the butter in the fish. Season with salt and pepper. If the mackerel are too big to fit inside the cooker, remove the heads.
2. Place each mackerel in a roasting bag and secure the end with a non-metallic tie. Prick each bag.
3. Place the mackerel side by side on a large plate with cut side facing up. Cook for 4 minutes.
4. Turn the mackerel over and turn the plate round. Cook for a further 4 minutes. Turn the mackerel again and turn the plate round. Cook for 4 minutes.
5. Leave to stand in the bags for 4 minutes. Serve garnished with lemon quarters and parsley.

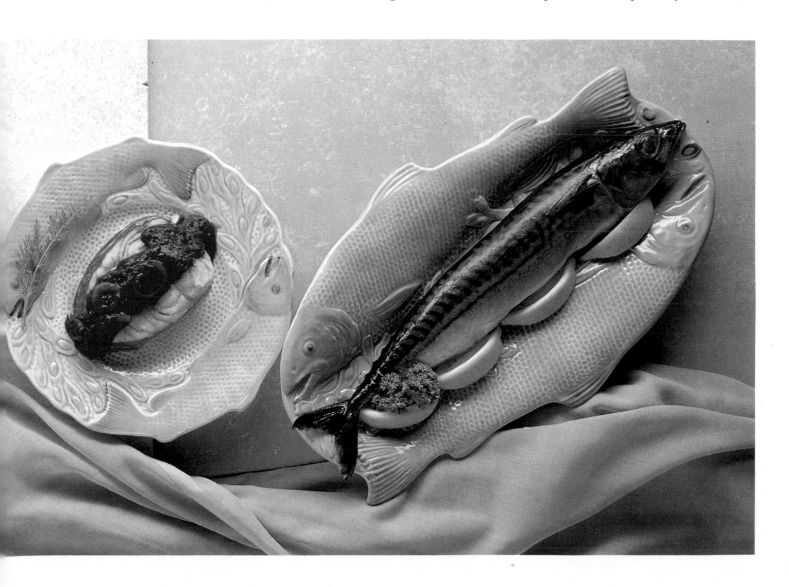

TUNA MOUSSE

*Preparation time: 10 minutes, plus setting Cooking time: 5 minutes
Microwave setting: Maximum (Full)*

25 g (1 oz) butter
25 g (1 oz) plain flour
300 ml ($\frac{1}{2}$ pint) cold chicken
    stock
$\frac{1}{4}$ teaspoon ground mace
15 g ($\frac{1}{2}$ oz) powdered
    gelatine
4 tablespoons dry sherry
300 ml ($\frac{1}{2}$ pint) mayonnaise
2 teaspoons anchovy
    essence

2 × 200 g (7 oz) cans tuna
    fish, drained and
    chopped
salt
freshly ground black
    pepper
150 ml ($\frac{1}{4}$ pint) double or
    whipping cream,
    whipped

To garnish:
slices of lemon
parsley sprigs

1. Place the butter in a 600 ml (1 pint) jug and cook for 1 minute or until melted.
2. Blend in the flour, stock and mace. Cook for a further 3$\frac{1}{2}$ minutes and set aside.
3. Place the gelatine in a small bowl and stir in the sherry. Cook for 3 seconds until dissolved. Stir to dissolve the gelatine completely.
4. Whisk the sherry gelatine liquid into the sauce. Set aside to cool slightly.
5. Stir the mayonnaise, anchovy essence, tuna fish, salt and pepper into the sauce. Fold in the cream.
6. Gently pour the mixture into a 1.2 litre (2 pint) prepared soufflé dish. Place in the refrigerator and chill for at least 4 hours or until set.
7. Turn out and garnish with lemon and parsley.

HADDOCK MOUSSE

*Preparation time: about 10 minutes, plus chilling
Cooking time: 6$\frac{1}{2}$–7$\frac{1}{2}$ minutes Microwave setting: Maximum (Full)*

450 g (1 lb) haddock fillets,
    cut into pieces
25 g (1 oz) aspic jelly
    powder
300 ml ($\frac{1}{2}$ pint) hot water
1 teaspoon dried parsley
salt
freshly ground black
    pepper

3 tablespoons double
    cream
2 egg whites

To garnish:
cucumber slices
watercress sprigs

1. Place the fillets in a medium bowl, cover and cook for 6–7 minutes. Rearrange halfway through. Set aside, covered.
2. Stir the aspic jelly into the hot water. Cook, uncovered, for 30 seconds. Stir well to dissolve.
3. Drain, skin and flake the fish. Stir in the aspic, parsley, salt and pepper to taste. Set aside until cold. Stir in the cream.
4. Whisk the egg whites until stiff. Gently fold into the fish mixture. Spoon into a 750 ml (1$\frac{1}{4}$ pint) ring mould. Chill until set. Serve with a garnish of cucumber and watercress.

Left: Tuna mousse; Haddock mousse. Right: Poached salmon; Fruit salad; Vichyssoise; Mixed green salad and potato salad

DINNER PARTY

Vichyssoise

Poached Salmon
Mixed Green Salad
Potato Salad

Fruit Salad

Order of Cooking
1. Prepare and cook Vichyssoise (page 19), Salmon, Potato Salad (page 111) and Fruit Salad (page 126) earlier in the day.
2. Prepare the mixed salad ingredients.

POACHED SALMON

Preparation time: about 3 minutes, plus cooling
Cooking time: about 12 minutes, plus standing
Microwave setting: Maximum (Full)

1 × 1.5 kg (3 lb) salmon   mayonnaise, to serve

1. Cover a large plate with clingfilm and place the salmon on the plate. Cover and cook for 12 minutes, rearranging halfway through cooking. Leave to stand, covered, for 5 minutes. Remove cover and leave to cool.
2. Pipe mayonnaise along length of salmon and serve with mixed green salad and potato salad.

BUTTERED JERUSALEM ARTICHOKES

Preparation time: about 10 minutes
Cooking time: about 9 minutes, plus standing
Microwave setting: Maximum (Full)

3 tablespoons water	40 g (1½ oz) butter, cut into
salt	pieces
450 g (1 lb) Jerusalem	1 tablespoon chopped
artichokes, peeled and	fresh parsley, to garnish
sliced	

1. Place the water, salt and artichokes in a large bowl. Cover and cook for 9 minutes, stirring halfway through cooking.
2. Leave to stand, covered, for 5 minutes.
3. Drain and toss in the butter. Garnish with parsley.

CROQUETTE POTATOES

Preparation time: about 10 minutes, plus standing and chilling
Cooking time: 11½–13 minutes Microwave setting: Maximum (Full)

3 tablespoons water	½ tablespoon milk
salt	freshly ground pepper
600 g (1¼ lb) potatoes,	1 egg, lightly beaten
peeled and chopped	75 g (3 oz) toasted
25 g (1 oz) butter	breadcrumbs

1. Place the water and salt in a large bowl. Add the potatoes, cover and cook for 9 minutes. Leave to stand, covered, for 5 minutes.
2. Beat the butter, milk and salt and pepper to taste into the potatoes. Roll the mixture into 16 cork shapes. Chill for 30 minutes for a firmer texture.
3. Coat the croquettes with egg and roll in breadcrumbs. Place on a piece of paper towel, in a circle. Prick with a fork. Cook, uncovered, for 2½–4 minutes, turning over halfway through cooking.

CAULIFLOWER CHEESE

Preparation time: about 10 minutes Cooking time: about 15 minutes
Microwave setting: Maximum (Full)

1 cauliflower, prepared	freshly ground black
weight 750 g (1½ lb)	pepper
	1 teaspoon made English
Sauce:	mustard
25 g (1 oz) butter	50 g (2 oz) Cheddar
25 g (1 oz) plain flour	cheese, grated
300 ml (½ pint) milk	chopped fresh parsley, to
salt	garnish

1. Rinse the cauliflower in water and place it in a medium bowl. Cover and cook for 10 minutes, turning the cauliflower over halfway through cooking. Keep hot while making the sauce.
2. Place the butter in a 600 ml (1 pint) jug. Cook for 1 minute or until melted.
3. Blend in the flour, milk, salt, pepper and mustard. Cook for 3 minutes, stirring every minute.
4. Stir in the cheese and cook for 1 minute.
5. Pour the sauce over the cauliflower and garnish with the parsley.

From left to right: Buttered Jerusalem artichokes; Croquette potatoes; Cauliflower cheese

VEGETABLES

CABBAGE WITH CARAWAY

Preparation time: about 5 minutes Cooking time: about 8 minutes
Microwave setting: Maximum (Full)

3 tablespoons water
salt
350 g (12 oz) cabbage, stalk
    removed and finely
    shredded

1 tablespoon caraway
    seeds
15 g (½ oz) butter

1. Place the water and salt in a large bowl. Place the cabbage on top. Cover and cook for 8 minutes. Halfway through cooking, stir in the caraway seeds.
2. Stir the butter into the cabbage until melted.

BOILED POTATOES

Preparation time: about 10 minutes
Cooking time: about 9 minutes, plus standing
Microwave setting: Maximum (Full)

3 tablespoons cold water
pinch of salt
4 potatoes, total weight
    750g (1½ lb), peeled and
    cut in half

25 g (1 oz) butter, cut into
    pieces
1 tablespoon chopped
    fresh parsley

1. Place the water and salt in a large bowl. Add the potatoes, cover and cook for 9 minutes, stirring halfway through cooking. Leave to stand, covered, for 8–10 minutes.
2. Drain off the water. Add the butter and parsley and toss to coat the potatoes.

PARSNIPS WITH PARSLEY

Preparation time: about 8 minutes
Cooking time: about 8 minutes, plus standing
Microwave setting: Maximum (Full)

3 tablespoons water
salt
1 tablespoon fresh
    chopped parsley

750 g (1½ lb) parsnips,
    peeled and quartered
15 g (½ oz) butter

1. Place the water, salt and parsley in a large bowl. Place the parsnips on top. Cover and cook for 8 minutes, stirring halfway through cooking.
2. Leave to stand, covered, for 5 minutes. Strain, then stir in the butter until melted.

MINTED PEAS

Preparation time: about 3 minutes Cooking time: about 7–9 minutes
Microwave setting: Maximum (Full)

3 tablespoons water
1 teaspoon fresh
    chopped mint

salt
450 g (1 lb) frozen peas
25 g (1 oz) butter, diced

1. Place the water, mint, salt and peas in a medium bowl. Cover and cook for 7–9 minutes, stirring halfway through cooking.
2. Drain the peas and toss in the butter.

Clockwise: Braised celery; Sweetcorn; Minted peas;
Parsnips with parsley; Green beans; Vichy carrots; Boiled
potatoes; Cabbage with caraway

BRAISED CELERY

Preparation time: about 5 minutes
Cooking time: about 11 minutes, plus standing
Microwave setting: Maximum (Full)

3 tablespoons water
salt
450 g (1 lb) head of celery,
    trimmed and stalks
    halved
1 medium onion, peeled
    and thinly sliced

150 ml (¼ pint) hot chicken
    stock
25 g (1 oz) butter, cut into
    pieces
1 teaspoon chopped fresh
    parsley
freshly ground pepper

1. Place the water and salt in an oblong or oval casserole dish. Place half the celery in the dish and spread over the onion. Cover the onion with the remaining celery. Cover and cook for 8 minutes. After 5 minutes of cooking, rearrange the vegetables.
2. Mix together the hot stock, butter, parsley, and salt and pepper to taste. Pour over the celery, cover and cook for 3 minutes. Leave to stand, covered, for 3–4 minutes before serving.

VICHY CARROTS

Preparation time: about 10 minutes Cooking time: about 6–9 minutes
Microwave setting: Maximum (Full)

3 tablespoons cold water
1 teaspoon caster sugar
450 g (1 lb) carrots, peeled
    and thinly sliced

25 g (1 oz) butter, cut into
    pieces
1 tablespoon chopped
    fresh parsley

1. Place the water, sugar and carrots in a medium bowl. Cover and cook for 6–9 minutes or until tender, stirring halfway through cooking.
2. Drain and stir in the butter until melted. Fold in the parsley. Serve hot. If serving with the Guard of Honour (page 63), stand covered until the corn has heated and then drain, and complete the recipe.

GREEN BEANS

Preparation time: about 2 minutes Cooking time: about 9 minutes, plus
standing Microwave setting: Maximum (Full)

450 g (1 lb) frozen whole
    green beans

salt

1. Place the beans in a medium bowl. Cover and cook for 9 minutes, stirring halfway through cooking. Leave to stand, covered, for 2 minutes. Drain off all excess water.
2. Sprinkle with salt and toss before serving.

SWEETCORN

Preparation time: about 3 minutes Cooking time: about 6 minutes
Microwave setting: Maximum (Full)

2 × 300 g (11½ oz) cans
    sweetcorn kernels,
    drained

25 g (1 oz) butter, cut into
    pieces

1. Place the sweetcorn in a casserole dish, cover and cook for 6 minutes, stirring halfway through.
2. Stir in the butter until melted.

CABBAGE PARCELS

Preparation time: about 15 minutes
Cooking time: about 13 minutes, plus standing
Microwave setting: Maximum (Full)

1 small, tight green cabbage, stalk removed	300 ml (½ pint) hot beef stock
1 medium onion, peeled and finely chopped	½ teaspoon Worcestershire sauce
225 g (8 oz) tomatoes, skinned and chopped	½ teaspoon dried mixed herbs
15 g (½ oz) butter	salt
4 tablespoons plain flour	freshly ground pepper
	4 tablespoons cooked rice

1. **Cook the whole cabbage conventionally** for 4 minutes in boiling salted water. Drain.
2. Gently peel off 8 leaves. Use the remaining cabbage in a vegetable soup.
3. Place the onion, tomatoes and butter in a medium bowl. Cover and cook for 4 minutes.
4. Stir in the flour, stock, Worcestershire sauce, herbs, salt, pepper and rice. Cook uncovered for 2 minutes.
5. Place a little of the mixture on each of the cabbage leaves. Fold the cabbage leaves over to make a parcel and tie with string.
6. Arrange the cabbage parcels in a shallow dish, cover and cook for 7 minutes, turning the dish round halfway through cooking.
7. Leave the cabbage parcels to stand for 5 minutes.

BROCCOLI WITH CHEESE SAUCE

Preparation time: about 10 minutes
Cooking time: about 11 minutes, plus standing
Microwave setting: Maximum (Full)

Frozen broccoli may be used instead of fresh.

3 tablespoons water	300 ml (½ pint) milk
salt	1 teaspoon made English mustard
450 g (1 lb) fresh broccoli, stalks halved lengthways	salt
chopped fresh parsley, to garnish (optional)	freshly ground black pepper
	50 g (2 oz) Cheddar cheese, grated

Sauce:
25 g (1 oz) butter
25 g (1 oz) plain flour

1. Place the water and salt in a large bowl. Arrange the broccoli in the bowl with stalks standing upwards. Cover with cling film and cook for 7 minutes. Set aside, covered.
2. Place the butter in a jug. Cook for 1 minute or until melted. Blend in the flour, milk, mustard and salt and pepper to taste. Cook for 3 minutes, stirring every minute. Stir in the cheese. Cook for 1 minute.
3. Pour the sauce over the drained broccoli and garnish with parsley (if using).

Above: Cabbage parcels;
Broccoli with cheese sauce.
Right: Stuffed onions; Stuffed
jacket potatoes

STUFFED ONIONS

Preparation time: about 25 minutes
Cooking time: about 14–16 minutes, plus standing
Microwave setting: Maximum (Full)

4 large onions, total weight 1 kg (2 lb), peeled	1 teaspoon Worcestershire sauce
25 g (1 oz) fresh white breadcrumbs	½ egg, lightly beaten
¼ teaspoon dried sage	salt
¼ teaspoon dried tarragon	freshly ground black pepper
¼ teaspoon dried parsley	15 g (½ oz) butter

1. Remove the centres from the onions, using a grapefruit knife, leaving shells about 2–3 layers deep. Set the shells aside, and chop the centres.
2. Mix the chopped onion with the breadcrumbs, sage, tarragon, parsley, Worcestershire sauce, egg, and salt and pepper to taste.
3. Stuff each onion with the breadcrumb mixture and top with a small knob of butter.
4. Arrange the onions in a circle on a plate and cook, uncovered, for 14–16 minutes, rearranging halfway through cooking. Leave to stand for 3 minutes before serving.

STUFFED JACKET POTATOES

Preparation time: about 10 minutes
Cooking time: about 16 minutes, plus standing
Microwave setting: Maximum (Full)

4 medium potatoes, washed and dried	15 g (½ oz) butter
75 g (3 oz) Cheddar cheese, grated	salt
1 tablespoon tomato purée	freshly ground black pepper
1 tablespoon Worcestershire sauce	chopped fresh parsley, to garnish

1. Place the potatoes on a paper towel, prick them and cook for 6 minutes.
2. Turn the potatoes over and turn the paper towel round. Cook for a further 7 minutes.
3. Wrap each potato tightly in foil and leave to stand for 5 minutes.
4. Cut a lengthways slice off the top of each potato. Scoop out the flesh, leaving the potato shell intact.
5. Mix the potato flesh with the cheese, tomato purée, Worcestershire sauce, butter, salt and pepper.
6. Pile the mixture back into the potato jackets and reheat for 3 minutes. Serve garnished with parsley.

COURGETTE SHELLS WITH BACON

Preparation time: about 10 minutes
Cooking time: about 12 minutes, plus standing
Microwave setting: Maximum (Full)

4 courgettes, halved
   lengthways
1 bacon rasher, rinds
   removed and chopped
1 small onion, peeled and
   finely chopped
1 teaspoon dried mixed
   herbs

25–50 g (1–2 oz) fresh
   white breadcrumbs
1 egg yolk
4 tablespoons stock
salt
freshly ground black
   pepper

1. Using a teaspoon, scoop the centres from the courgette halves. Set the shells aside, and chop the scooped-out flesh; there should be about 25 g (1 oz).
2. Place the courgette flesh, bacon, onion and herbs in a small bowl. Cover and cook for 3 minutes. Stir in the breadcrumbs, egg yolk, stock, and salt and pepper to taste.
3. Fill one half of each courgette shell with the stuffing. Replace the other half and secure with wooden cocktail sticks.
4. Place in a shallow dish, cover and cook for 9 minutes, rearranging halfway through cooking. Leave to stand for 3–4 minutes before serving.

STUFFED MARROW

Preparation time: 20 minutes
Cooking time: about 30½ minutes, plus grilling
Microwave setting: Maximum (Full)

1 medium marrow, about
   750 g (1½ lb), halved and
   seeds removed
1 medium onion, peeled
   and finely chopped
1 small carrot, peeled and
   grated
2 tomatoes, skinned and
   chopped
1 teaspoon dried mixed
   herbs
75 g (3 oz) fresh brown
   breadcrumbs
350 g (12 oz) minced beef

1 teaspoon Worcestershire
   sauce
1 tablespoon tomato purée
salt
freshly ground black
   pepper

Sauce:
25 g (1 oz) butter
25 g (1 oz) plain flour
300 ml (½ pint) milk
salt
freshly ground black
   pepper

1. Place the marrow halves in a shallow dish. Cover and cook for 14 minutes.
2. Drain the marrow, cover and set aside.
3. Place the onion, carrot, tomatoes and herbs in a large bowl. Cover and cook for 5 minutes.
4. Stir in the breadcrumbs, meat, Worcestershire sauce, tomato purée, salt and pepper. Cover and cook for 4 minutes. Set aside.
5. To make the sauce, place the butter in a 600 ml (1 pint) jug. Cook for 1 minute or until melted.
6. Blend in the flour, milk, salt and pepper. Cook for 3 minutes, stirring every minute.
7. Fill the marrow halves with the stuffing. Spoon over the sauce, and cook for 3½ minutes.
8. **Brown under a preheated conventional grill** before serving if liked.

Clockwise: Peppers with savoury rice; Stuffed aubergines; Stuffed marrow; Courgette shells with bacon

PEPPERS WITH SAVOURY RICE

Preparation time: about 10 minutes
Cooking time: about 29 minutes, plus standing
Microwave setting: Maximum (Full)

1 onion, peeled and finely chopped	salt
25 g (1 oz) butter	freshly ground pepper
50 g (2 oz) ham, finely chopped	100 g (4 oz) long-grain rice
1 garlic clove, peeled and crushed	450 ml (¾ pint) hot beef stock
1 tablespoon tomato purée	4 green peppers, cored, seeded and blanched
1 teaspoon dried mixed herbs	

1. Place the onion, butter, ham, garlic, tomato purée, herbs, salt and pepper in a large bowl. Cover and cook for 4 minutes.
2. Stir in the rice and hot stock, cover and cook for 9 minutes.
3. Leave to stand, covered, for about 10 minutes.
4. Stand the peppers in a casserole. Stuff the peppers with the rice, cover and cook for 5 minutes.
5. Turn the casserole round and cook for 5 minutes.
6. Leave the peppers to stand, covered, for 5 minutes before serving.

STUFFED AUBERGINES

Preparation time: 20 minutes, plus salting
Cooking time: about 18¼ minutes
Microwave setting: Maximum (Full)

2 medium aubergines, about 250 g (9 oz) each	1 tablespoon chopped fresh parsley
salt	2 teaspoons Worcestershire sauce
oil, for brushing	dash of Angostura bitters (optional)
1 medium onion, peeled and finely chopped	1 garlic clove, peeled and crushed
4 streaky bacon rashers, rinds removed, diced	freshly ground pepper
50 g (2 oz) mushrooms, chopped	75 g (3 oz) brown breadcrumbs
100 g (4 oz) butter	50 g (2 oz) Cheddar cheese, finely grated
2 tablespoons tomato purée	

1. Cut the aubergines in half lengthways. Sprinkle the cut edges with salt and set aside. After 30 minutes, rinse them with cold water and pat dry.
2. Scoop out the flesh and dice it. Brush shell with oil.
3. Place the onion in a large bowl. Cover and cook for 2½ minutes. Stir in the bacon and diced aubergines. Cover and cook for 4 minutes.
4. Stir in the mushrooms, butter, tomato purée, chopped parsley, Worcestershire sauce, Angostura bitters (if using), garlic, salt and pepper. Cover and cook for 3 minutes. Leave to stand, covered.
5. Place the aubergine shells on a plate or shallow casserole dish, cover and cook for 2 minutes. Turn each shell around, cover and cook for 2 minutes.
6. Stir the breadcrumbs into the stuffing. Spoon the stuffing into the shells. Cook for 2 minutes.
7. Sprinkle the grated cheese on top. Cook for 45 seconds or until the cheese has melted.

VEGETARIAN CURRY

Preparation time: about 20 minutes Cooking time: about 19 minutes
Microwave setting: Maximum (Full)

1 tablespoon vegetable oil	25 g (1 oz) dark brown
1 small green pepper,	sugar
cored, seeded and finely	2 tablespoons curry
chopped	powder
2 carrots, peeled and finely	2 teaspoons turmeric
sliced	2 tablespoons desiccated
1 celery stick, finely	coconut
chopped	25 g (1 oz) plain flour
2 large onions, peeled and	300 ml (½ pint) hot
finely chopped	vegetable stock
3 tomatoes, skinned and	2 tablespoons sultanas
chopped	25 g (1 oz) peanuts
1 tablespoon lemon juice	salt
1 large eating apple,	freshly ground black
peeled, cored and	pepper
chopped	

1. Place the oil, green pepper, carrots and celery in a bowl. Cover and cook for 5 minutes.
2. Stir in the onions, tomatoes, lemon juice, apple, sugar, curry powder, turmeric and coconut. Cover and cook for 10 minutes, stirring halfway through cooking.
3. Stir in the flour, hot stock, sultanas, peanuts, salt and pepper. Cover and cook for 4 minutes, stirring halfway through cooking.
4. Serve with brown rice.

ONION & POTATO BAKE

Preparation time: about 12 minutes Cooking time: about 14 minutes
Microwave setting: Maximum (Full)

450 g (1 lb) onions, peeled	2 teaspoons dried mixed
and thinly sliced	herbs
600 g (1¼ lb) potatoes,	scant 75 ml (3 fl oz) milk
peeled and thinly sliced	parsley sprigs, to garnish
salt	
freshly ground black	
pepper	

1. Place the onions in a medium bowl, cover and cook for 5 minutes, stirring halfway through cooking.
2. Layer the potatoes and onions in a 1.2 litre (2 pint) casserole dish. Sprinkle each layer with a little salt, pepper and herbs. Finish with a layer of potatoes. Pour in the milk.
3. Stand the dish on a plate. Cover and cook for 9 minutes, turning round halfway through cooking.
4. Garnish with a sprig of parsley.

Clockwise: Salami and tomato pizza; Potato salad; Onion and potato bake; Vegetarian curry

SALAMI AND TOMATO PIZZA

Preparation time: about 20 minutes, plus rising
Cooking time: about 11 minutes Microwave setting: Maximum (Full)

Serves 4–6

50 ml (2 fl oz) milk	350 g (12 oz) fresh
10 g (¼ oz) dried yeast	tomatoes, skinned and
pinch of caster sugar	chopped, or 350 g (12 oz)
25 g (1 oz) butter	canned tomatoes
1 egg, beaten	1 tablespoon dried
175 g (6 oz) plain flour,	oregano
sifted with a pinch of salt	salt
	freshly ground black
	pepper
Topping:	75–100 g (3–4 oz) salami,
1 garlic clove, peeled and	thinly sliced
crushed	75 g (3 oz) Cheddar
1 medium onion, peeled	cheese, grated
and finely chopped	6 anchovies, drained
15 g (½ oz) butter	6 stuffed green olives,
2 tablespoons tomato	halved
purée	

1. Place the milk in 300 ml (½ pint) jug. Cook for 15 seconds. Sprinkle the yeast and sugar over the milk and leave to stand for 10 minutes, or until frothy.
2. Place the butter in a small bowl. Cook for 45 seconds or until melted.
3. Pour the yeast mixture, melted butter and egg into the flour and salt. Knead for 10 minutes or until smooth. Shape into a ball and place in a bowl.
4. Cover and cook for 30 seconds. Leave covered for 10 minutes.
5. Remove the cover and leave dough to rise until it has doubled in size; this will take about 20 minutes.
6. To make the topping, place the garlic, onion and butter in a medium bowl. Cover and cook for 3 minutes. Stir in the tomato purée, tomatoes, oregano, salt and pepper. Cook for 2 minutes. Set aside.
7. Knead the dough and roll it out to make a 23 cm (9 inch) circle. Place on a plate and cook for 2½ minutes.
8. Spread the tomato and onion topping over the pizza base and cover with the salami slices and grated cheese. Arrange the anchovies on top in a lattice pattern. Garnish with halved olives. Cook for 2 minutes and serve straightaway.

POTATO SALAD

Preparation time: about 10 minutes, plus cooling
Cooking time: 9–10 minutes Microwave setting: Maximum (Full)

3 tablespoons water	200 ml (7 fl oz) mayonnaise
salt	1 tablespoon chopped
750 g (1½ lb) potatoes,	fresh chives, to garnish
peeled and cut into 1 cm	
(½ inch) cubes	

1. Place the water and salt in a large bowl. Place the potatoes on top. Cover and cook for 9–10 minutes, stirring halfway through cooking.
2. Leave to stand, covered, for 15 minutes. Remove the cover and gently stir with a fork to separate the potato cubes. Leave to stand until cold.
3. Stir in the mayonnaise and sprinkle with chives.

BOILED RICE

Preparation time: about 3 minutes
Cooking time: about 13 minutes, plus standing
Microwave setting: Maximum (Full)

225g (8 oz) long-grain rice   salt
750 ml (1¼ pints) boiling   ¼ teaspoon oil
  chicken stock

1. Place the rice in a large bowl. Stir in the boiling stock, salt and oil. Cover and cook for 13 minutes, stirring halfway through cooking.
2. Leave to stand, covered, for 10 minutes before fluffing up with a fork.

From left to right: Boiled rice;
Spaghetti all'uova; Buttered
spaghetti; Cooked lentils

BUTTERED SPAGHETTI

Preparation time: about 3 minutes   Cooking time: about 9 minutes, plus
standing   Microwave setting: Maximum (Full)

salt   225 g (8 oz) spaghetti
1 tablespoon oil   100 g (4 oz) butter, cut into
1.75 litres (3 pints) boiling   pieces
  water

1. Place the salt, oil and water in a large bowl. Stand the spaghetti in the water and cook, uncovered, for 1 minute.
2. Gently push the remaining spaghetti under the water. Cover and cook for 8 minutes. Check during cooking that all the spaghetti is completely submerged.
3. Leave to stand, covered, for 10 minutes. Drain and toss in the butter.

RICE, PASTA & PULSES

SPAGHETTI ALL'UOVA

Preparation time: about 8 minutes Cooking time: about 9 minutes, plus standing Microwave setting: Maximum (Full)

225 g (8 oz) spaghetti
salt
1 tablespoon oil
1.75 litres (3 pints) boiling
  water

3 eggs, lightly beaten
100 g (4 oz) butter, cut into
  pieces
50 g (2 oz) pecorino
  cheese, grated

1. Cook the spaghetti in the salt, oil and water as in Buttered Spaghetti (see left).
2. Leave to stand, covered, for 10 minutes. Drain and toss in the beaten eggs until set.
3. Place half the butter in a serving bowl. Pile in the spaghetti and dot with the remaining butter.
4. Serve sprinkled with the grated cheese.

COOKED LENTILS

Preparation time: about 3 minutes
Cooking time: 21 minutes, plus standing
Microwave setting: Maximum (Full) and Defrost

225 g (8 oz) red split lentils

50 g (2 oz) butter, cut into
  pieces

1. Place the lentils in a medium bowl with cold water to cover. Cover and cook at Maximum for 6 minutes or until boiling.
2. Turn to Defrost and cook for 15 minutes. Stand, covered, for 10 minutes before serving.
3. Drain and toss in butter.

KEDGEREE

Preparation time: about 15 minutes
Cooking time: about 20 minutes, plus standing
Microwave setting: Maximum (Full)

750 g (1½ lb) smoked cod or haddock fillets
350 g (12 oz) long-grain rice
750 ml (1¼ pints) hot chicken stock
salt
¼ teaspoon oil
50 g (2 oz) butter, cut into cubes
1 egg, beaten

2 hard-boiled egg whites, chopped
freshly ground black pepper
1 tablespoon single cream

To garnish:
chopped fresh parsley
1 hard-boiled egg white, chopped
1 hard-boiled egg yolk, sieved

1. Place the cod or haddock in a shallow dish. Cover and cook for 3½ minutes. Turn the dish round and cook for a further 3½ minutes.
2. Flake the fish and set aside.
3. Place the rice, hot stock, salt and oil into a large bowl. Cover and cook for 12 minutes.
4. Leave to stand, covered, for 7 minutes.
5. Stir the flaked fish into the rice with the butter, beaten egg, chopped egg whites, pepper and cream. Cover and cook for 4 minutes, stirring halfway through cooking.
6. Garnish with the chopped parsley, chopped egg white and sieved egg yolk, arranged decoratively over the kedgeree.

CURRIED RICE

Preparation time: about 10 minutes
Cooking time: 18 minutes, plus standing
Microwave setting: Maximum (Full)

1 large onion, peeled and finely chopped
1 garlic clove, peeled and crushed
50 g (2 oz) sultanas
2 tablespoons tomato purée
1 tablespoon mild curry powder
1 teaspoon mild chilli powder

1 teaspoon dried mixed herbs
salt
¼ teaspoon oil
350 g (12 oz) long-grain rice
750 ml (1¼ pints) boiling beef stock
bay leaves, to garnish

1. Place the onion in a large bowl, cover and cook for 5 minutes, stirring halfway through cooking.
2. Stir in the garlic, sultanas, tomato purée, curry powder, chilli powder, herbs, salt, oil, rice and stock. Cover and cook for 13 minutes. Leave to stand, covered, for 10 minutes.
3. Fluff the rice with a fork. Serve garnished with bay leaves.

Clockwise; Risotto; Paella; Curried rice; Kedgeree

RISOTTO

Preparation time: about 15 minutes
Cooking time: about 23 minutes, plus standing
Microwave setting: Maximum (Full)

50 g (2 oz) butter
1 large onion, peeled and
 finely chopped
¼ green pepper, cored,
 seeded and finely diced
¼ red pepper, cored,
 seeded and finely diced
1 tablespoon tomato purée
1 garlic clove, peeled and
 crushed
1 teaspoon dried mixed
 herbs
50 g (2 oz) mushrooms,
 finely chopped

400 g (14 oz) long-grain
 rice
750 ml (1¼ pints) hot
 chicken stock
100 g (4 oz) ham, finely
 chopped
¼ teaspoon oil
salt
freshly ground black
 pepper
1 tablespoon chopped
 fresh parsley, to garnish

1. Place the butter, onion, peppers, tomato purée, garlic, herbs and mushrooms in a large bowl. Cover and cook for 8 minutes, stirring halfway through cooking.
2. Stir in the rice, stock, ham, oil, salt, pepper, then cover and cook for 15 minutes, stirring halfway through cooking.
3. Remove from the cooker and leave to stand, covered, for 8 minutes.
4. Stir the risotto with a fork, and sprinkle with chopped parsley. Hand grated Parmesan cheese separately, and serve with a mixed green salad.

PAELLA

Preparation time: about 15 minutes
Cooking time: about 30 minutes, plus standing
Microwave setting: Maximum (Full)

1 large onion, peeled and
 chopped
2 garlic cloves, peeled and
 crushed
350 g (12 oz) long-grain
 rice
750 ml (1¼ pints) boiling
 chicken stock
few strands of saffron
salt
¼ teaspoon oil

100g (4 oz) frozen peas
175 g (6 oz) cooked peeled
 prawns
175 g (6 oz) cooked
 mussels
175 g (6 oz) cooked cockles
100 g (4 oz) cooked chicken
 meat, diced
2 tomatoes, peeled and
 chopped
cooked prawns in shells, to
 garnish

1. Place the onion and garlic in a large bowl, cover and cook for 6½ minutes, stirring halfway through.
2. Stir the rice, stock, saffron, salt and oil into the onion. Cover and cook for 13 minutes, stirring halfway through cooking. Set aside, covered, for 13 minutes.
3. Meanwhile place the peas in a medium bowl, cover and cook for 3½ minutes. Stir in the prawns, mussels, cockles, chicken and tomatoes. Cover and cook for 7½ minutes, stirring halfway through cooking. Drain and stir into the rice.
4. Serve hot, garnished with prawns.

SPAGHETTI BOLOGNESE

Preparation time: about 20 minutes Cooking time: about 20½ minutes
Microwave setting: Maximum (Full)

1 quantity cooked
 spaghetti (see page 112)
4 streaky bacon rashers,
 rinds removed, chopped
1 medium onion, peeled
 and finely chopped
2 garlic cloves, peeled and
 crushed
1 celery stick, finely
 chopped
1 small carrot, peeled and
 grated
25 g (1 oz) plain flour
225 g (8 oz) minced beef

450 g (1 lb) tomatoes,
 skinned and chopped, or
 1 × 400 g (14 oz) can
 tomatoes
4 tablespoons tomato
 purée
300 ml (½ pint) hot beef
 stock
100 g (4 oz) mushrooms,
 chopped
salt
freshly ground black
 pepper
2 teaspoons dried mixed
 herbs

1. Cook the spaghetti in the salt, oil and water as in Buttered Spaghetti (see page 112).
2. Place the bacon, onion, garlic, celery and carrot in a bowl. Cover and cook for 7½ minutes, stirring halfway through.
3. Stir in the flour, beef, tomatoes and tomato purée. Cover and cook for 3 minutes.
4. Stir in the stock, mushrooms, salt, pepper and herbs. Cover. Cook for 10 minutes, stirring after 5.

STUFFED CANNELLONI

Preparation time: about 10 minutes.
Cooking time: about 24½ minutes, plus standing
Microwave setting: Maximum (Full)

Stuffing:
1 small onion, peeled and
 finely chopped
1 garlic clove, peeled and
 crushed
1 teaspoon dried mixed
 herbs
225 g (8 oz) minced meat
2 tablespoons tomato
 purée
salt
freshly ground black
 pepper

Sauce:
1 small onion, peeled and
 finely chopped
1 garlic clove, peeled and
 crushed
1 teaspoon dried mixed
 herbs
25 g (1 oz) butter, cut into
 pieces
25 g (1 oz) plain flour
1 × 400 g (14 oz) can
 tomatoes
2 tablespoons tomato
 purée
8 cannelloni tubes

1. To make the stuffing, place the onion, garlic and herbs in a bowl. Cover and cook for 4 minutes.
2. Stir in the meat, tomato purée, and salt and pepper. Cover and cook for 5 minutes, stirring halfway through. Set aside, covered.
3. Place the onion, garlic and herbs in a medium bowl. Cover and cook for 4 minutes.
4. Stir in the butter until melted. Stir in the flour. Blend in the tomatoes and their liquid, tomato purée, and salt and pepper to taste. Cook, uncovered, for 3½ minutes, stirring halfway through cooking. Purée.
5. Stuff the cannelloni tubes with the meat stuffing. Place in a 1.2 litre (2 pint) casserole dish.
6. Pour over sauce. Cook, covered, for 12 minutes.
7. Leave to stand for 3–4 minutes before serving.

HAM & CHICKEN LASAGNE

Preparation time: about 15 minutes, plus standing Cooking time: about
34¼ minutes, plus grilling Microwave setting: Maximum (Full)

1 × 350 g (12 oz) chicken
 portion
175 g (6 oz) green lasagne
½ teaspoon oil
900 ml (1½ pints) boiling
 water
salt
1 medium onion, peeled
 and finely chopped
1 small green pepper,
 cored, seeded and finely
 chopped

40 g (1½ oz) butter
40 g (1½ oz) plain flour
300 ml (½ pint) milk
150 ml (¼ pint) hot chicken
 stock
50 g (2 oz) cooked ham,
 finely chopped
freshly ground black
 pepper
40 g (1½ oz) Cheddar
 cheese, finely grated

1. Place the chicken in a shallow dish. Cover and cook for 6 minutes. Set aside, covered, for 5 minutes. Discard skin and bones, chop flesh. Set aside.
2. Place the lasagne in a 5 cm (2 inch) deep oblong casserole dish. Pour over the oil, boiling water and salt, completely covering the lasagne with water. Cover and cook for 9 minutes.
3. Set aside, covered, for 15 minutes. Drain the lasagne and place it on a separate plate.
4. Place the onion, green pepper and butter in a medium bowl. Cover and cook for 7 minutes.
5. Sprinkle in the flour and gradually stir in the milk. Cook for 4 minutes. Blend in the hot stock. Stir in the chicken, ham, salt and pepper. Cook for 2 minutes.
6. Place half the drained lasagne in a layer at the bottom of the casserole dish. Pour over half the sauce. Place the remaining lasagne over the sauce and cover with the remaining sauce. Sprinkle the cheese on top and cook for 1¼ minutes or until the cheese has melted.
7. **Brown under a preheated conventional grill.**

MACARONI CHEESE

Preparation time: about 10 minutes Cooking time: about 23–25 minutes
plus grilling Microwave setting: Maximum (Full)

1.2 litres (2 pints) boiling
 water
¼ teaspoon oil
225 g (8 oz) macaroni

Sauce:
50 g (2 oz) butter
50 g (2 oz) plain flour

600 ml (1 pint) milk
½ teaspoon prepared
 English mustard
salt
freshly ground black
 pepper
150 g (5 oz) Cheddar
 cheese, finely grated

1. Place the water, oil and macaroni in a large bowl. Cover and cook for 15 minutes. Set aside, covered.
2. Place the butter in a jug. Cook, uncovered, for 1 minute or until the butter has melted. Stir in the flour, then blend in the milk, mustard and salt and pepper to taste. Cook, uncovered, for 5–7 minutes, stirring every minute.
3. Stir in 75 g (3 oz) of the cheese. Drain the macaroni and fold into the cheese sauce. Pour into a casserole.
4. Sprinkle over the remaining cheese. Cook, uncovered, for 2 minutes, or until the cheese has melted. Or, if desired, **brown under a preheated conventional grill.**

Clockwise: Spaghetti bolognese; Macaroni cheese; Stuffed cannelloni; Ham and chicken lasagne

APPLE & SULTANA SUET PUDDING

Preparation time: about 20 minutes
Cooking time: about 11 minutes, plus standing
Microwave setting: Maximum (Full)

Serves 4–6

150 g (5 oz) shredded suet
½ teaspoon baking powder
250 g (9 oz) self-raising
   flour
150 ml (¼ pint) water
25 g (1 oz) fresh brown
   breadcrumbs

100 g (4 oz) soft dark brown
   sugar
2 teaspoons ground
   cinnamon
100 g (4 oz) sultanas
600 g (1¼ lb) cooking
   apples, peeled, cored
   and thinly sliced

1. Place the suet, baking powder and flour in a bowl. Mix together. Gradually add water to make pastry.
2. Roll out two thirds of the pastry to 3 mm (⅛ inch) thick and line a greased 1.5 litre (2½ pint) basin.
3. Mix together the breadcrumbs, sugar, cinnamon and sultanas.
4. Starting and ending with the apples, make alternate layers with the breadcrumb mixture.
5. Roll out the remaining pastry and cover the filling, making sure the pastry lid is well sealed. Make 2 cuts in the lid.
6. Cover with cling film, allowing sufficient room for rising. Cook for 5 minutes. Turn the basin round and cook for a further 6 minutes.
7. Leave to stand, covered, for 5 minutes before turning out and serving.

PUDDINGS & CAKES

APPLE & BLACKBERRY CRUMBLE

Preparation time: about 20 minutes
Cooking time: about 9 minutes, plus standing and grilling
Microwave setting: Maximum (Full)

Serves 4–6

600 g (1¼ lb) cooking
   apples, peeled, cored
   and thinly sliced
350 g (12 oz) blackberries
75 g (3 oz) sugar

175 g (6 oz) plain flour
75 g (3 oz) soft dark brown
   sugar
75 g (3 oz) butter

1. Make alternate layers with the apples,
blackberries and sugar in a casserole.
2. Mix the flour and dark brown sugar together, then
rub in the butter until the mixture resembles fine
breadcrumbs. Sprinkle the mixture over the fruit.
3. Cook for 9 minutes. Leave the crumble to stand for
3 minutes before serving. **Brown under a preheated
conventional grill.**

TREACLE PUDDING

Preparation time: about 10 minutes
Cooking time: about 4 minutes, plus standing
Microwave setting: Maximum (Full)

3 tablespoons golden
  syrup
100 g (4 oz) self-raising
  flour
50 g (2 oz) shredded suet
50 g (2 oz) caster sugar

1 egg
2 tablespoons water
4 tablespoons milk
2 drops vanilla essence

1. Place the golden syrup in the bottom of a lightly greased 900 ml (1½ pint) basin.
2. Mix the flour, suet and sugar together. Beat in the egg, water, milk and vanilla essence. Spoon the mixture on to the syrup in the basin.
3. Cover the basin with cling film and cook for 2 minutes. Remove the cling film and turn the basin round. Cook for a further 2 minutes.
4. Leave the pudding to stand for 2 minutes before turning out and serving.

COLD STRAWBERRY SOUFFLÉ

Preparation time: about 15 minutes, plus setting
Cooking time: about 15 seconds Microwave setting: Maximum (Full)

Serves 6

2 tablespoons white wine
4 tablespoons water
1 tablespoon powdered
  gelatine
300 ml (½ pint) strawberry
  purée
1½ tablespoons lemon juice
100 g (4 oz) caster sugar

300 ml (½ pint) double
  cream, stiffly whipped
6 egg whites, stiffly
  whisked

To decorate:
150 ml (¼ pint) double or
  whipping cream, stiffly
  whipped
6 strawberries

1. Place the wine, water and gelatine in a small jug. Stir together well and cook for 30 seconds. Stir to ensure the gelatine has dissolved.
2. Add the strawberry purée, lemon juice and sugar to the gelatine mixture and stir well. Allow to cool, stirring once or twice.
3. Carefully fold the cream into the strawberry mixture, then gently fold in the egg whites.
4. Tie greaseproof paper around the outside of 6 individual ramekin dishes so that it extends 1.5 cm (½ inch) above the rim. Spoon the soufflé mixture into the ramekin dishes.
5. Chill until set, then remove the paper and decorate each soufflé with piped whipped cream and a strawberry.

Treacle pudding; Cold
strawberry soufflé

CHRISTMAS PUDDING

Preparation time: about 15 minutes Cooking time: about 10 minutes, plus standing Microwave setting: Maximum (Full)

75 g (3 oz) plain flour	75 g (3 oz) sultanas
¼ teaspoon salt	100 g (4 oz) raisins
75 g (3 oz) shredded suet	40 g (1½ oz) blanched
½ teaspoon mixed spice	almonds, chopped
¼ teaspoon ground	50 g (2 oz) chopped apple
cinnamon	juice of ½ lemon
40 g (1½ oz) fresh white	grated rind of ½ lemon
breadcrumbs	4 tablespoons brandy
50 g (2 oz) caster sugar	2 eggs
50 g (2 oz) mixed peel	50 ml (2 fl oz) milk
50 g (2 oz) molasses sugar	2 teaspoons cane syrup
50 g (2 oz) glacé cherries,	2 teaspoons gravy
chopped	browning
75 g (3 oz) currants	

This pudding tastes best when freshly made. As it only takes 10 minutes to cook, it is easily fitted in to the Christmas lunch schedule, see page 89. Do not put any silver pieces or coins into the mixture. Be careful not to overcook the mixture and be in attendance throughout the operation. It is also advisable not to reheat the pudding in the microwave cooker.

1. Mix all the dry ingredients together, then stir in the liquids.
2. Place the mixture in a 1 kg (2 lb) greased pudding basin. Cover the basin and cook for 5 minutes.
3. Leave to stand for 5 minutes, then cook for a further 5 minutes.
4. Allow the pudding to stand for 5 minutes.

QUEEN OF PUDDINGS

Preparation time: about 15 minutes
Cooking time: about 10½ minutes, plus grilling
Microwave setting: Maximum (Full)

3 egg yolks	grated rind of ½ lemon
50 g (2 oz) caster sugar	2 tablespoons jam
600 ml (1 pint) milk	
2 drops vanilla essence	**Topping:**
175 g (6 oz) fresh white	175 g (6 oz) caster sugar
breadcrumbs	3 egg whites, stiffly
	whisked

1. Place the egg yolks, caster sugar, milk and vanilla essence in a 1 litre (1¾ pint) jug and whisk together. Cook for 4 minutes.
2. Place the breadcrumbs and grated lemon rind in a 1.2 litre (2 pint) casserole and stir in the milk mixture. Cook for 5½ minutes, stirring halfway through cooking. Set aside.
3. Place the jam in a small dish. Cook for 1 minute.
4. Gently spread the jam over the cooked breadcrumb and milk mixture.
5. For the topping, fold the sugar into the whisked egg whites. Spread the meringue over the jam and swirl into decorative peaks.
6. **Brown the pudding under a preheated conventional grill.**

Christmas pudding;
Queen of puddings

FRUIT STUFFED PANCAKES

Preparation time: about 35 minutes
Cooking time: about 10 minutes, plus standing
Microwave setting: Maximum (Full)

1 egg
1 egg yolk
300 ml (½ pint) milk
100 g (4 oz) plain flour
pinch of salt
oil, for frying

Filling:
175 g (6 oz) dried apricots
hot water
2 drops almond essence
juice of 1 lemon
50 g (2 oz) ground almonds
2 tablespoons caster sugar
2 tablespoons icing sugar,
    sifted

1. Beat together the egg, egg yolk and milk.
2. Sift the flour and salt into a large bowl. Make a well in the centre and gradually incorporate the egg and milk mixture into the flour to make a batter.
3. **Using a conventional hob**, heat a little of the oil in a 15 cm (6 inch) frying pan. Pour a small amount of batter into the pan, swirling the batter round. Cook until golden.
4. Make 8 pancakes in this way. Set the pancakes aside while you make the filling.
5. Place the apricots in a bowl and cover with hot water. Cover and cook for 5 minutes. Leave the apricots to stand, covered, for 20 minutes.
6. Drain the apricots, pour into a liquidizer and blend until smooth.
7. Mix together the apricot purée, almond essence, lemon juice, ground almonds and caster sugar. Spread a little of the purée in the centre of each pancake and roll up.
8. Arrange 4 pancakes on a plate and cook for 2½ minutes. Repeat with the remaining pancakes.
9. Sprinkle with icing sugar before serving.

BAKED STUFFED APPLES

Preparation time: about 15 minutes
Cooking time: 14 minutes, plus standing
Microwave setting: Maximum (Full)

3 tablespoons mincemeat
3 tablespoons strawberry
    jam
1 teaspoon ground
    cinnamon

4 large cooking apples,
    total weight 1.25 kg (2¾
    lb), cored, skin scored
    around middle

1. Mix the mincemeat, jam and cinnamon together.
2. Stand the apples in a shallow dish. Spoon the filling into the cavities in the apples.
3. Cook for 7 minutes. Turn the dish round and cook for a further 7 minutes or until tender.
4. Leave the apples to stand for 4 minutes before serving.

Fruit stuffed pancakes; Baked
stuffed apples

MIXED FRUIT SPONGE PUDDING

Preparation time: about 10 minutes
Cooking time: about 6 minutes, plus standing
Microwave setting: Maximum (Full)

100 g (4 oz) butter
100 g (4 oz) caster sugar
2 eggs
175 g (6 oz) self-raising
   flour

2 tablespoons water
50 g (2 oz) mixed dried
   fruit

1. Cream the butter and sugar together until light and fluffy.
2. Beat in the eggs one at a time, then carefully fold in the flour. Stir in the water and dried fruit.
3. Place the mixture in a greased 1.2 litre (2 pint) bowl. Cover and cook for 6 minutes, turning halfway through cooking.
4. Remove the cover and leave the pudding to stand for 2 minutes before turning it out. Serve hot.

HONEY CHEESECAKE

Preparation time: about 10 minutes, plus chilling
Cooking time: about 3 minutes Microwave setting: Maximum (Full)

Serves 6

1 tablespoon golden syrup
100 g (4 oz) butter
225 g (8 oz) digestive
   biscuits, crushed
350 g (12 oz) full-fat soft
   cheese
$\frac{1}{2}$ teaspoon ground
   cinnamon
1 tablespoon lemon juice
2 tablespoons water

1 tablespoon powdered
   gelatine
4 tablespoons clear honey
150 ml ($\frac{1}{4}$ pint) double
   cream, whipped

To decorate:
150 ml ($\frac{1}{4}$ pint) double or
   whipping cream,
   whipped
walnut halves

1. Place the syrup and butter in a medium bowl. Cook for $1\frac{1}{4}$ minutes.
2. Stir in the crushed biscuits and mix well. Use this mixture to line a 20 cm (8 inch) flan case.
3. Beat the cheese and cinnamon together until smooth.
4. Place lemon juice and water in a 600 ml (1 pint) jug and stir in the gelatine. Cook for 15 seconds. Stir well to make sure the gelatine has dissolved.
5. Place the honey in another 600 ml (1 pint) jug. Cook for 30 seconds. Pour the honey into the first jug containing the gelatine and mix well together. Allow to cool slightly.
6. Beat the honey mixture into the cheese mixture and fold in the whipped cream. Spoon into the flan case and chill until set.
7. Decorate the cheesecake with the whipped cream and walnut halves.

Mixed fruit sponge pudding;
Honey cheesecake

CHOCOLATE MOUSSE

Preparation time: about 10 minutes, plus setting
Cooking time: about 2 minutes Microwave setting: Maximum (Full)

Serves 6

6 slices jam Swiss roll	4 egg yolks
4 tablespoons Grand Marnier	4 egg whites, stiffly whisked
225 g (8 oz) milk chocolate, broken into pieces	**To decorate:**
25 g (1 oz) butter	150 ml ($\frac{1}{4}$ pint) double or whipping cream, stiffly whipped
1 tablespoon cold strong black coffee	1 tablespoon grated chocolate
1 tablespoon brandy	

1. Place 1 slice of Swiss roll into the base of each of 6 small dishes. Sprinkle with the Grand Marnier.
2. Place the chocolate in a medium bowl. Cook for 2 minutes or until it has melted.
3. Beat in the butter, coffee, brandy and egg yolks. Gently fold in the egg whites.
4. Spoon the mousse over the Swiss roll and smooth over the top. Chill until set.
5. Decorate each dish with swirls of cream and grated chocolate.

PINEAPPLE FLAN

Preparation time: about 20 minutes, plus setting
Cooking time: about 2$\frac{1}{2}$ minutes Microwave setting: Maximum (Full)

Serves 4–6

100 g (4 oz) butter	50 g (2 oz) white marshmallows
1 tablespoon golden syrup	300 ml ($\frac{1}{2}$ pint) double cream, whipped
225 g (8 oz) gingernut biscuits, crushed	
4 tablespoons pineapple juice	**To decorate:**
15 g ($\frac{1}{2}$ oz) powdered gelatine	glacé cherries
1 × 400 g (14 oz) can crushed pineapple, drained	pieces of crystallized angelica

1. Place the butter and syrup in a medium bowl. Cook for 1$\frac{1}{4}$ minutes.
2. Stir in the crushed biscuits and mix well. Use this mixture to line a 20 cm (8 inch) flan case.
3. Place the pineapple juice into a 600 ml (1 pint) jug and stir in the gelatine. Cook for 10 seconds, then stir until the gelatine has dissolved.
4. Place the crushed pineapple and marshmallows in a medium bowl. Cook for 1 minute or until the marshmallows have melted.
5. Whisk the pineapple juice and gelatine mixture into the pineapple and marshmallow mixture. Leave until almost set.
6. Fold the cream into the pineapple mixture and then spoon into the flan case, smoothing the top.
7. Decorate the flan with the cherries and angelica. Chill until set. Serve chilled.

TRIFLE

Preparation time: about 15 minutes, plus cooling
Cooking time: about 5$\frac{1}{2}$ minutes Microwave setting: Maximum (Full)

Serves 6

6 trifle sponges, cut into pieces	3 eggs
12 ratafia biscuits, crumbled	1 egg yolk
150 ml ($\frac{1}{4}$ pint) sweet sherry	150 ml ($\frac{1}{4}$ pint) double or whipping cream, whipped
50 ml (2 fl oz) orange juice	1 egg white, stiffly whisked
4 tablespoons strawberry jam	**To decorate:**
25 g (1 oz) caster sugar	chopped nuts
400 ml (14 fl oz) milk	angelica

1. Divide the sponges between 6 glass dishes or 1 large dish. Sprinkle the ratafia biscuits over the sponge.
2. Mix the sherry and orange juice together and pour over the sponge ratafia base. Spread a little strawberry jam over the soaked base.
3. Place the caster sugar and milk in a small bowl. Cook for 2 minutes.
4. Whisk the eggs and egg yolk together, then pour the heated milk on to the eggs, whisking all the time. Cook for 3$\frac{1}{2}$ minutes. Check and whisk the custard every 30 seconds.
5. Whisk and strain the custard before spooning it over the soaked sponge bases. Leave to cool.
6. Fold the cream and egg white together. Gently spread the cream over the custard and decorate the trifle with chopped nuts and angelica.

PINEAPPLE UPSIDE DOWN PUDDING

Preparation time: about 15 minutes
Cooking time: about 7$\frac{1}{2}$ minutes, plus standing
Microwave setting: Maximum (Full)

165 g (5$\frac{1}{2}$ oz) butter	100 g (4 oz) caster sugar
25 g (1 oz) soft dark brown sugar	2 eggs
3 slices canned pineapple	100 g (4 oz) self-raising flour, sifted
4 glacé cherries	

1. Use 15 g ($\frac{1}{2}$ oz) of the butter to grease a 1.2 litre (2 pint) soufflé dish.
2. Place 25 g (1 oz) of the butter and the brown sugar in the dish and cook for 1 minute.
3. Arrange the pineapple slices and cherries in the base of the dish in a decorative pattern.
4. Beat the remaining butter and caster sugar together until light and fluffy.
5. Beat in the eggs and fold in the flour. Gently spread this over the pineapple and cherries.
6. Cook for 3 minutes, turn the dish round and cook for further 3$\frac{1}{2}$ minutes.
7. Leave the pudding to stand for 3 minutes before turning out.

Clockwise: Trifle; Chocolate mousse; Pineapple upside down pudding; Pineapple flan

FRESH FRUIT SALAD

Preparation time: about 30 minutes, plus cooling and standing
Cooking time: about 5 minutes Microwave setting: Maximum (Full)

100 g (4 oz) sugar
150 ml (¼ pint) water
1 tablespoon lemon juice
1 tablespoon Grand
  Marnier
50 g (2 oz) white grapes,
  peeled, halved and
  deseeded
50 g (2 oz) black grapes,
  peeled, halved and
  deseeded
1 dessert apple, peeled,
  cored, quartered and
  thinly sliced

1 dessert pear, peeled,
  cored and sliced
1 large orange, peeled and
  segmented
1 paw paw, peeled,
  deseeded and diced
¼ honeydew melon, skin
  removed, deseeded and
  diced
1 kiwi fruit, peeled and
  sliced
1 banana, peeled and
  sliced

1. Place the sugar and water in a jug and cover. Heat for 5 minutes, then stir and leave to cool.
2. When the syrup is cool, stir in the lemon juice and Grand Marnier.
3. Place all the prepared fruit into a large glass bowl. Pour the syrup over the fruit.
4. Leave for 1 hour to let the flavours mingle.

BAKED BANANAS

Preparation time: about 10 minutes Cooking time: about 4 minutes
Microwave setting: Maximum (Full)

4 bananas, peeled and
  sliced
4 tablespoons rum
4 tablespoons orange juice

50 g (2 oz) ginger biscuits,
  crushed
40 g (1½ oz) soft brown
  sugar
150 ml (¼ pint) double
  cream

1. Place the sliced bananas in a glass dish.
2. Mix the rum and orange juice together and pour over the bananas.
3. Mix the biscuits and sugar together and sprinkle over the bananas.
4. Cover the dish and cook for 2 minutes. Turn the dish round and cook for a further 2 minutes.
5. Uncover and pour the cream over the baked bananas. Serve at once.

From left to right: Fresh fruit
salad; Baked bananas;
Lemon meringue pie;
Ginger sponge pudding

LEMON MERINGUE PIE

Preparation time: about 20 minutes
Cooking time: about 10 minutes, plus browning
Microwave setting: Maximum (Full)

175 g (6 oz) prepared shortcrust pastry	25 g (1 oz) cornflour
finely grated rind of 2 lemons	200 g (7 oz) caster sugar
	2 egg yolks, beaten
125 ml (4 fl oz) lemon juice	2 egg whites, stiffly whisked

1. Roll out the pastry and use it to line a 15 cm (6 inch) pie dish. Prick the pastry all over with a fork and cook for 5 minutes, or until crisp.
2. Make up the lemon rind and juice with cold water to 300 ml (½ pint).
3. Mix the cornflour in a 600 ml (1 pint) jug with a little of the lemon water, then gradually stir in the remaining liquid. Cook for 3½ minutes or until the mixture thickens, stirring every minute.
4. Whisk 75 g (3 oz) of the sugar with the egg yolks. Beat into the lemon mixture. Pour into the pastry case and leave to cool.
5. Place the whisked egg whites in a bowl and fold in the remaining sugar. Pile over the lemon filling. Cook for 1½ minutes.
6. **Place under a preheated conventional grill** to lightly brown the meringue.

GINGER SPONGE PUDDING

Preparation time: about 10 minutes
Cooking time: about 6 minutes, plus standing
Microwave setting: Maximum (Full)

100 g (4 oz) butter	2 teaspoons ground ginger
100 g (4 oz) caster sugar	5 pieces preserved ginger, drained and sliced
2 eggs	
100 g (4 oz) self-raising flour, sifted	

1. Cream the butter and sugar together until light and fluffy.
2. Beat in the eggs, one at a time, then fold in the sifted flour and ground ginger.
3. Arrange the sliced ginger over the base of a greased 900 ml (1½ pint) bowl. Spoon the pudding mixture over the ginger in the bowl, smoothing the top.
4. Cover and cook for 3 minutes. Turn the bowl round and cook for a further 3 minutes.
5. Remove the cover and leave the pudding to stand for 2 minutes before turning it out. Serve hot with Egg Custard (page 139) or Orange Sauce (page 139).

CHOCOLATE BANANA RING

Preparation time: about 10 minutes, plus cooling
Cooking time: about 9 minutes, plus standing
Microwave setting: Maximum (Full)

2 eggs
4 tablespoons milk
150 g (5 oz) soft brown sugar
100 g (4 oz) soft margarine
450 g (1 lb) bananas, peeled and chopped
225 g (8 oz) self-raising flour

½ teaspoon baking powder
40 g (1½ oz) drinking chocolate powder

Icing:
50 g (2 oz) icing sugar
40 g (1½ oz) drinking chocolate
1 tablespoon water

1. Place the eggs, milk, sugar, margarine and bananas into a liquidizer and blend until smooth.
2. Sift the flour, baking powder and drinking chocolate into a large bowl. Stir in the banana mixture and mix thoroughly until well combined.
3. Spoon the mixture into a 2.25 litre (4 pint) greased microwave baking ring. Cook for 6 minutes.
4. Gently spread any uncooked cake mixture over the surface. Turn round and cook for 3 minutes.
5. Leave the ring to stand for 5 minutes before turning it out. Leave to cool completely.
6. Mix the sifted icing sugar and drinking chocolate together. Quickly stir in the water. Spread the glacé icing over the top of the cake, drizzling some down the sides of the cake.

ONE STAGE CHOCOLATE CAKE

Preparation time: about 10 minutes, plus cooling
Cooking time: about 9 minutes, plus standing
Microwave setting: Maximum (Full)

Makes one 18 cm (7 inch) cake

175 g (6 oz) soft margarine
175 g (6 oz) caster sugar
40 g (1½ oz) cocoa powder
150 g (5 oz) self-raising flour
1 teaspoon baking powder

2 drops vanilla essence
3 tablespoons milk
3 eggs
2 tablespoons icing sugar, to decorate

1. Place all the ingredients, except the icing sugar, in a large bowl. Beat well until the mixture is smooth, but be careful not to overbeat.
2. Spoon the mixture into a greased and bottom-lined 18 cm (7 inch) round, 9 cm (3½ inch) deep container. Stand the container on an upturned plate and cook for 3 minutes.
3. Turn the container round and cook for a further 3 minutes. Turn round again and cook for 2½ minutes.
4. Leave the cake to stand for 5 minutes before turning it out. Leave to cool completely.
5. Turn the cake out upside down on to a serving plate and sift icing sugar over the top to decorate.

LEMON SPONGE CAKE

Preparation time: about 10 minutes, plus cooling
Cooking time: about 5 minutes, plus standing
Microwave setting: Maximum (Full)

Makes one 18 cm (7 inch) cake

225 g (8 oz) self-raising flour
¼ teaspoon baking powder
100 g (4 oz) butter
100 g (4 oz) soft dark brown sugar
2 eggs
2 teaspoons grated lemon rind
1 tablespoon milk

2 teaspoons lemon juice
3 tablespoons Lemon Curd (page 132)
225 g (8 oz) icing sugar, sifted
2 tablespoons water
yellow food colouring
8 sugared lemon slices, to decorate

1. Sift the flour and baking powder into a large bowl. Rub in the butter until the mixture resembles breadcrumbs, then stir in the sugar.
2. Beat in the eggs, one at a time, then stir in the lemon rind, milk and lemon juice.
3. Spoon the mixture into a greased and lined 18 cm (7 inch) round, 9 cm (3½ inch) deep container. Stand on an upturned plate and cook for 2 minutes.
4. Turn the container round and cook for a further 2 minutes. Turn round again and cook for 1 minute.
5. Leave the sponge to stand for 5 minutes before turning it out upside down on to a serving plate. Leave to cool completely.
6. Split the cake into 2 layers. Spread one layer with the lemon curd and replace the other layer on top.
7. Mix the icing sugar with the water and yellow food colouring. Pour over the cake and decorate with lemon slices.

GINGERBREAD

Preparation time: about 10 minutes
Cooking time: about 5 minutes, plus standing
Microwave setting: Maximum (Full)

50 g (2 oz) treacle
15 g (½ oz) caster sugar
50 g (2 oz) butter
100 g (4 oz) plain flour, sifted

½ teaspoon bicarbonate of soda
½ teaspoon ground mixed spice
½ teaspoon ground ginger
1 egg (size 1)

1. Place the treacle, sugar and butter in a medium bowl. Cook for 1½ minutes.
2. Allow the mixture to cool slightly, then stir in the sifted flour, bicarbonate of soda, mixed spice and ginger. Beat in the egg.
3. Pour into a greased 900 ml (1½ pint) deep oblong plastic container. Stand on an upturned plate and cook for 1 minute.
4. Turn the container round and cook for 1 minute. Turn it round again and cook for 1½ minutes.
5. Allow the gingerbread to stand for 5 minutes before turning out. Serve cut in slices and buttered.

Clockwise: Lemon sponge cake; Gingerbread; One stage chocolate cake; Chocolate banana ring

MULLED RED WINE

Preparation time: about 5 minutes Cooking time: about 4 minutes
Microwave setting: Maximum (Full)

Makes just over 750 ml (1¼ pints)

450 ml (¾ pint) red wine
150 ml (¼ pint) water
150 ml (¼ pint) orange juice
25 g (1 oz) caster sugar

4 tablespoons brandy
½ teaspoon ground
    cinnamon
8 orange slices, to decorate

1. Place the wine, water, orange juice, sugar, brandy and cinnamon in a jug. Stir well and pour into 4 tumblers.
2. Heat for 4 minutes, stirring halfway through.
3. Decorate with the orange slices.

MULLED CIDER

Preparation time: about 5 minutes Cooking time: about 4 minutes
Microwave setting: Maximum (Full)

Makes just over 750 ml (1¼ pints)

450 ml (¾ pint) dry cider
150 ml (¼ pint) apple juice
150 ml (¼ pint) orange juice

25 g (1 oz) caster sugar
½ teaspoon ground mixed
    spice
8 apple slices

1. Place the cider, apple juice, orange juice, sugar and mixed spice into a large jug. Stir well and pour into 4 tumblers.
2. Place an apple slice in each tumbler. Heat for 4 minutes, stirring halfway through heating.
3. Decorate with the remaining apple slices.

From left to right: Mulled cider;
Hot rum punch; Mulled red wine

DRINKS & PRESERVES

HOT RUM PUNCH

Preparation time: about 5 minutes Cooking time: about 10 minutes
Microwave setting: Maximum (Full)

450 ml (¾ pint) water
1 orange
6 cloves
2 Ceylon tea bags
rind of ½ lemon
1 cinnamon stick
150 ml (¼ pint) dark rum

150 ml (¼ pint) white wine
150 ml (¼ pint) orange juice
50 g (2 oz) soft dark brown
  sugar

To decorate:
4 small slices orange
4 small slices lemon

1. Place the water in a large jug and cook for 5 minutes.
2. Stud the orange with the cloves and add to the water with the tea bags, lemon rind and cinnamon stick. Stir and cover, then set aside for 5 minutes, removing the tea bags after 3 minutes.
3. Place the rum, wine, orange juice and brown sugar in a jug. Cook for 5 minutes, stirring halfway through cooking.
4. Remove the orange and cloves, rind and cinnamon stick. Strain. Mix the tea and rum mixtures together, then pour into 4 heatproof or warmed glasses. Place a small slice of lemon and orange in each glass.

STRAWBERRY JAM

Preparation time: about 5 minutes, plus cooling
Cooking time: about 26 minutes Microwave setting: Maximum (Full)

Makes about 450 g (1 lb)

450 g (1 lb) strawberries   350 g (12 oz) sugar
1 tablespoon lemon juice

1. Place the strawberries and lemon juice in a large bowl. Cover and cook for 6 minutes or until the strawberries are soft.
2. Stir in the sugar. Cook uncovered for a further 20 minutes or until setting point is reached, stirring halfway through cooking.
3. Allow the jam to cool before spooning into clean, dry jars. Seal and label.

LEMON CURD

Preparation time: about 10 minutes Cooking time: about 6 minutes
Microwave setting: Maximum (Full)

Makes about 450 g (1 lb)

100 g (4 oz) butter   grated rind of 3 large
225 g (8 oz) sugar   lemons
6 tablespoons lemon juice   3 eggs, beaten

1. Place the butter, sugar, lemon juice and rind in a large bowl. Cook, uncovered, for 3 minutes, stirring halfway through cooking.
2. Beat the eggs into the mixture. Cook for 5 minutes or until the lemon curd thickens, checking and stirring every minute.
3. Allow the lemon curd to cool before spooning into clean, dry jars. Seal and label.

From left to right: Strawberry jam; Lemon curd; Gooseberry jam; Tomato chutney

GOOSEBERRY JAM

Preparation time: about 10 minutes, plus cooling
Cooking time: about 30 minutes Microwave setting: Maximum (Full)

Makes about 750 g (1½ lb)

200 ml (7 fl oz) water
450 g (1 lb) gooseberries,
  topped and tailed

450 g (1 lb) sugar

1. Place the water and gooseberries in a large bowl. Cover and cook for 5 minutes.
2. Stir the jam and remove the cover. Cook for a further 5 minutes or until the gooseberries are soft.
3. Stir in the sugar. Cook uncovered for 20 minutes or until setting point is reached, stirring halfway through cooking.
4. Allow the jam to cool before spooning into clean, dry jars. Seal and label.

TOMATO CHUTNEY

Preparation time: about 10 minutes Cooking time: about 34 minutes
Microwave setting: Maximum (Full)

Makes about 1.5 kg (3 lb)

350 g (12 oz) tomatoes,
  skinned and chopped
350 g (12 oz) cooking
  apples, peeled, cored
  and sliced
1 medium onion, peeled
  and finely chopped

350 g (12 oz) raisins
2 teaspoons salt
2 teaspoons mixed spice
1 garlic clove, peeled and
  crushed
225 g (8 oz) molasses sugar
450 ml (¾ pint) malt vinegar

1. Place the tomatoes, apples and onion in a large bowl. Cover and cook for 10 minutes, stirring halfway through cooking.
2. Stir in the raisins, salt, mixed spice, garlic, sugar and vinegar. Cook for 24 minutes, stirring the chutney several times during cooking.
3. Allow the chutney to cool before spooning into clean, dry jars. Seal and label.

HOT CHOCOLATE

Preparation time: about 5 minutes Cooking time: about 8½ minutes
Microwave setting: Maximum (Full)

Makes 750 ml (1¼ pints)

50 g (2 oz) plain chocolate,   5 marshmallows, chopped
  broken into pieces
600 ml (1 pint) milk

1. Place the chocolate in a large jug. Heat for 3½
minutes or until the chocolate has melted.
2. Stir in the milk and heat for 4 minutes.
3. Whisk in the marshmallows until they have
melted. Heat for 1 minute, then pour into 4 warmed
mugs or glasses.

HOT WHISKY EGG NOG

Preparation time: about 5 minutes Cooking time: about 6 minutes
Microwave setting: Maximum (Full)

750 ml (1¼ pints) milk   2 eggs, lightly beaten
65 ml (2½ fl oz) whisky   1 teaspoon grated nutmeg,
50 g (2 oz) caster sugar   to decorate

1. Place the milk, whisky and sugar in a large jug.
Cook for 6 minutes, stirring halfway through.
2. Beat the eggs into the hot milk mixture. Strain into
4 heatproof or warmed tumblers. Sprinkle grated
nutmeg over each and serve immediately.

Hot chocolate; Hot whisky egg
nog; Calypso coffee, Orange tea

CALYPSO COFFEE

Preparation time: about 5 minutes Cooking time: about 4½ minutes
Microwave setting: Maximum (Full)

Makes 600 ml (1 pint)

600 ml (1 pint) cold, strong black coffee	4 tablespoons rum
25 g (1 oz) caster sugar	150 ml (¼ pint) double cream

1. Place the coffee, sugar and rum in a large jug. Heat for 4½ minutes, stirring halfway through.
2. Pour the coffee into 4 warmed glasses or cups.
3. Pour a little cream on the top of each coffee.

ORANGE TEA

Preparation time: about 10 minutes Cooking time: about 8 minutes
Microwave setting: Maximum (Full)

250 ml (8 fl oz) orange juice	**To decorate:**
600 ml (1 pint) water	4 slices orange
1 tablespoon caster sugar	4 mint sprigs
2 tea bags	

1. Place the orange juice, water and sugar in a large jug. Cook for 8 minutes, stirring halfway through cooking.
2. Stir in the tea bags, cover and leave to stand for 4 minutes.
3. Stir the orange tea, remove the tea bags, then pour into the 4 glasses and float a slice of orange on the top. Decorate each glass with a sprig of mint.

WHITE SAUCE

Preparation time: about 10 minutes, plus infusing
Cooking time: about 6 minutes Microwave setting: Maximum (Full)

Makes 300 ml (½ pint)

300 ml (½ pint) milk
1 small onion, peeled and
   stuck with 6 cloves
½ carrot, peeled and sliced
½ celery stick, chopped

25 g (1 oz) butter
25 g (1 oz) plain flour
salt
freshly ground black
   pepper

1. Place the milk, onion, carrot and celery in a medium bowl and cook for 3 minutes.
2. Leave to infuse for 10 minutes before straining.
3. Place the butter in a 600 ml (1 pint) jug and cook for 30 seconds or until melted.
4. Stir in the flour and gradually blend in the strained milk. Cook for 2½ minutes, stirring every minute, until thick and smooth.
5. Stir in the salt and pepper to taste.

Variations:

Egg Sauce: Add 1 finely chopped hard-boiled egg. Serve with vegetables and fish.

Cheese Sauce: Stir 25–75 g (1–3 oz) grated Cheddar cheese into the sauce until it melts. Season with 1 teaspoon made English mustard. Serve with vegetables, pasta, and fish.

Parsley Sauce: Add 1 tablespoon chopped fresh parsley. Serve with boiled bacon or fish.

Fish Sauce: Add 2 tablespoons cooked peeled prawns, ½ teaspoon lemon juice or anchovy essence and a pinch of paprika. Serve with vegetables or fish.

Caper Sauce: Add 1 tablespoon chopped capers and 1 tablespoon caper juice. Serve with boiled chicken or fish.

From left to right: White sauce;
Caper sauce; Egg sauce; Fish
sauce; Parsley sauce; Cheese
sauce

SAUCES

Clockwise from top: Orange sauce; Gooseberry sauce; Apple sauce;
Melba sauce; Chocolate custard; Jam sauce. Centre: Egg custard

JAM SAUCE

Preparation time: about 5 minutes Cooking time: about 3 minutes
Microwave setting: Maximum (Full)

Makes 175 ml (6 fl oz)

4 tablespoons jam
1 tablespoon lemon juice

4 tablespoons water

1. Place the jam, juice and water in a 600 ml (1 pint) jug. Cook for 3 minutes, stirring halfway through.
2. Sieve the sauce if necessary.
Serve with rice pudding.

EGG CUSTARD

Preparation time: about 10 minutes Cooking time: about 2 minutes
Microwave setting: Maximum (Full)

Makes 400 ml (14 fl oz)

300 ml (½ pint) milk
2 drops vanilla essence
1 egg

1 egg yolk
50 g (2 oz) caster sugar
25 g (1 oz) plain flour

1. Place the milk and vanilla essence in a 600 ml (1 pint) jug and cook for 2 minutes.
2. Place the egg, egg yolk and sugar in a medium bowl and beat together. Add the flour and beat until smooth. Gradually stir the milk into the egg mixture.
3. Gradually stir the milk into the egg mixture.
4. Cook the custard for 2 minutes, whisking every 30 seconds, until thick and smooth.
Serve with steamed sponge pudding.

CHOCOLATE CUSTARD

Preparation time: about 5 minutes Cooking time: about 2½ minutes
Microwave setting: Maximum (Full)

Makes 300 ml (½ pint)

15 g (½ oz) cornflour
15 g (½ oz) cocoa powder
25 g (1 oz) caster sugar

300 ml (½ pint) milk
15 g (½ oz) butter

1. Place the cornflour, cocoa powder and sugar in a 600 ml (1 pint) jug. Gradually blend in the milk.
2. Cook the custard for 2½ minutes, stirring every minute, until thick and smooth.
3. Beat in the butter and serve.

MELBA SAUCE

Preparation time: about 10 minutes, plus cooling
Cooking time: about 2½ minutes Microwave setting: Maximum (Full)

Makes 250 ml (8 fl oz)

350 g (12 oz) raspberries, sieved
3 tablespoons caster sugar

2 teaspoons cornflour
1 tablespoon water
½ teaspoon lemon juice

1. Place the raspberries and sugar in a 600 ml (1 pint) jug.
2. Blend the cornflour with the water and stir into the raspberries. Cook for 2½ minutes, stirring every minute.
3. Stir in the lemon juice, and allow to cool.
Serve with ice cream.

ORANGE SAUCE

Preparation time: about 10 minutes Cooking time: about 3½ minutes
Microwave setting: Maximum (Full)

Makes 400 ml (14 fl oz)

75 g (3 oz) butter
175 g (6 oz) icing sugar, sifted
175 ml (6 fl oz) concentrated orange juice

15 g (½ oz) cornflour
grated rind of 1 orange
1 egg, separated

1. Place the butter in a medium bowl, and cook for 1 minute or until melted. Beat the icing sugar into the melted butter.
2. Blend the orange juice and cornflour together and stir into the sugar mixture. Beat in the orange rind and egg yolk.
3. Cook for 2½ minutes or until thickened, stirring every 30 seconds.
4. Whisk the egg white into the orange sauce.
Serve with marmalade pudding or Ginger Sponge Pudding (page 127).

GOOSEBERRY SAUCE

Preparation time: about 10 minutes Cooking time: about 9 minutes
Microwave setting: Maximum (Full)

Makes 450 ml (¾ pint)

400 g (14 oz) gooseberries, topped and tailed
150 ml (¼ pint) water

25 g (1 oz) cornflour
50 g (2 oz) caster sugar

1. Place the gooseberries and 125 ml (4 fl oz) of the water in a large bowl. Cover and cook for 6 minutes, stirring halfway through cooking.
2. Rub through a sieve or blend in a liquidizer until smooth.
3. Blend together the cornflour and remaining water. Stir into the gooseberries. Stir in the sugar and cook, uncovered, for 3 minutes, stirring halfway through.
This is the classic accompaniment to grilled mackerel.

APPLE SAUCE

Preparation time: about 10 minutes Cooking time: about 5 minutes
Microwave setting: Maximum (Full)

Makes 200 ml (7 fl oz)

2 tablespoons water
grated rind of ½ small lemon
1 tablespoon caster sugar

15 g (½ oz) butter
450 g (1 lb) cooking apples, peeled, cored and finely sliced

1. Place the water, lemon rind, sugar, butter and apples in a large bowl. Cover and cook for 5 minutes, stirring halfway through cooking. Cool the sauce slightly.
2. Pour into a liquidizer and blend until smooth.
3. Return to the bowl and reheat for 3 minutes.
Serve with roast pork.

SAUCE BÉARNAISE

Preparation time: about 5 minutes Cooking time: about 1¾ minutes
Microwave setting: Maximum (Full)

Makes 150 ml (¼ pint)

75 g (3 oz) butter	salt
2 tablespoons tarragon vinegar	freshly ground black pepper
1 shallot, peeled and finely chopped	2 egg yolks (size 1 or 2)

To prevent curdling, check the sauce frequently during cooking. Serve with grilled steak.
1. Place the butter in a 600 ml (1 pint) jug and cook for 1 minute or until melted.
2. Whisk the tarragon vinegar, shallot, salt, pepper and egg yolks into the butter. Cook for 30 seconds, whisking the sauce every 15 seconds.
3. As soon as the sauce is ready, place the jug in cold water to prevent further cooking.

CURRY SAUCE

Preparation time: about 10 minutes Cooking time: about 12½ minutes
Microwave setting: Maximum (Full)

1 medium onion, peeled and chopped	¼ teaspoon ground ginger
1 garlic clove, peeled and crushed	¼ teaspoon grated nutmeg
1 medium apple, peeled, cored and chopped	1½ tablespoons plain flour
	1 tablespoon tomato purée
1 tablespoon ground coriander	1 teaspoon lemon juice
	¼ teaspoon meat extract
1 teaspoon turmeric	2 teaspoons curry paste
½ teaspoon ground cumin	450 ml (¾ pint) hot stock
¼ teaspoon chilli powder	salt
¼ teaspoon ground cinnamon	freshly ground black pepper

1. Place the onion, garlic, apple, coriander, turmeric, cumin, chilli powder, cinnamon, ginger and nutmeg in a medium bowl. Cover and cook for 4½ minutes, stirring halfway through cooking.
2. Stir in the flour, tomato purée, lemon juice, meat extract, curry paste, stock, and salt and pepper to taste. Cover and cook for 8–13 minutes, stirring halfway through cooking.

ONION SAUCE

Preparation time: about 10 minutes Cooking time: about 6½ minutes
Microwave setting: Maximum (Full)

Makes 300 ml (½ pint)

225 g (8 oz) onions, peeled and finely chopped	150 ml (¼ pint) milk
	salt
15 g (½ oz) butter	freshly ground black pepper
10 g (¼ oz) cornflour	

1. Place the onions and butter in a medium bowl, cover and cook for 5 minutes, stirring after 2.
2. Blend the cornflour with a little of the milk. Stir into the remaining milk, and add to the onions. Add the salt and pepper.
3. Cover and cook for 1½ minutes stirring once.

BREAD SAUCE

Preparation time: about 10 minutes
Cooking time: about 7 minutes, plus standing
Microwave setting: Maximum (Full)

1 medium onion, peeled and stuck with 8 cloves	50 g (2 oz) butter, cut into pieces
about 300 ml (½ pint) milk	salt
75 g (3 oz) fresh white breadcrumbs	freshly ground white pepper

1. Place the onion, 300 ml (½ pint) milk, breadcrumbs, butter, and salt and pepper to taste in a medium bowl. Cover and cook for 5 minutes. Leave to stand, covered, for 15 minutes.
2. Remove the onion and add 2 more tablespoons of milk to thin, if necessary. Cook, uncovered, for 2 minutes longer, stirring halfway through cooking. Serve with roast chicken.

CRANBERRY SAUCE

Preparation time: about 3 minutes, plus chilling
Cooking time: about 14 minutes
Microwave setting: Maximum (Full) and Defrost

175 g (6 oz) fresh cranberries	grated rind of 1 orange
	3 tablespoons orange juice
100 g (4 oz) caster sugar	

1. Place the cranberries, sugar, and orange rind and juice in a small bowl. Cover and cook on Maximum for 4 minutes.
2. Stir the mixture, re-cover and cook on Defrost for 10 minutes, stirring halfway through cooking.
3. Purée in a blender or food processor. Chill. Serve with roast turkey.

TOMATO SAUCE

Preparation time: about 15 minutes, plus cooling
Cooking time: about 13 minutes Microwave setting: Maximum (Full)

Makes 600 ml (1 pint)

25 g (1 oz) butter	2 tablespoons tomato purée
1 onion, peeled and finely chopped	25 g (1 oz) plain flour
1 garlic clove, peeled and crushed	600 g (1¼ lb) tomatoes, skinned and chopped
salt	freshly ground black pepper
1 teaspoon caster sugar	150 ml (¼ pint) hot chicken stock
1 teaspoon dried oregano	

1. Place the butter, onion, garlic, salt, sugar, oregano and tomato purée in a large bowl. Cover and cook for 5 minutes.
2. Stir in the flour, tomatoes and pepper, then cover and cook for a further 5 minutes.
3. Stir in the hot stock. Cool the sauce slightly.
4. Pour into a liquidizer and blend until smooth.
5. Sieve the sauce. Return to the bowl and reheat for 3 minutes before serving.
Serve with hamburgers, chops, sausages and fish.

Clockwise from top: Sauce Béarnaise; Bread sauce; Tomato sauce; Onion sauce; Curry sauce. Centre: Cranberry sauce

Acknowledgements

Photography: Peter Myers, except for pp 2-3, 4-5, 6, 26, 37, 43, 44: Charlie Stebbings
Photographic styling: Alison Williams and Paula Lovell
Preparation of food for photography: Michelle Thomson, Jennie Reekie and Margot Mason

The publishers would also like to thank the following companies for the loan of props for photography:
Astrohome, 47/49 Neal Street, London WC2
Graham and Greene, 7 Elgin Crescent, London W11
David Mellor, 26 James Street, London WC2 and 4 Sloane Square, London SW1
World's End Tiles, 9 Langton Street, London SW10

Microwave Cooker supplied by Toshiba UK Ltd, Toshiba House, Frimley Road, Frimley, Camberley, Surrey.
Food Chart details by Belling & Co. Ltd., Enfield, Middlesex